High Interest
Easy Reading

D1315705

NCTE Committee to Revise *High Interest—Easy Reading*

Patricia Phelan, University of San Diego, chair
Judy Beckman, University of Northern Iowa
Anne M. Bingley, Vista High School, Vista, California
Sharon Boyette, Bell Junior High School, San Diego, California
Meijean Chan, San Diego Unified School District, California
Cynthia Hedges, Point Loma High School, San Diego, California
Carol Jago, Santa Monica High School, Santa Monica, California
Brady Kelso, Scripps Ranch High School, San Diego, California
Madelon McGowan, Grossmont High School District, El Cajon, California
Susan Thompson, Crawford High School, San Diego, California
Christine Wells, El Capitan High School, Lakeside, California
Charlene Williams, Slater Elementary School, Fresno, California
Claudia Williams, Jackson-Olin High School, Birmingham, Alabama
Warren Williams, Chula Vista Junior High School, Chula Vista, California
Dawn Boyer, NCTE staff liaison

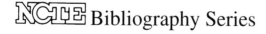 Bibliography Series

High Interest Easy Reading

An Annotated Booklist for Middle School and Senior High School

Seventh Edition

Patricia Phelan, Editor,
and the Committee to Revise
High Interest—Easy Reading
of the National Council of Teachers of English

National Council of Teachers of English
1111 W. Kenyon Road, Urbana, Illinois 61801-1096

Manuscript Editor: Jane M. Curran

Production Editor: Peter Feely

Cover Design: R. Maul

Interior Design: Tom Kovacs for TGK Design

NCTE Stock Number 20989-3050

ISBN 0-8141-2098-9

ISSN 1051-4740

About the NCTE Bibliography Series

The National Council of Teachers of English is proud to be part of a process that we feel is important. It begins when an educator who knows literature and its value to students and teachers is chosen by the NCTE Executive Committee to be a booklist editor. That editor then works with teachers and librarians who review, select, and annotate hundreds of new trade books sent to them by publishers. It's a complicated process, one that can last three or four years. But because of their dedication and strong belief in the need to let others know about the good literature that's available, these professionals volunteer their time in a way that serves as an inspiration to all of us. The members of the committee that compiled this volume are listed on one of the first pages, and we are grateful for their hard work.

In our bibliography series are five different booklists, each focused on a particular audience, each updated regularly. These are *Adventuring with Books* (pre-K through grade 6), *Kaleidoscope* (multicultural literature, grades K through 8), *Your Reading* (middle school/junior high), *Books for You* (senior high), and *High Interest—Easy Reading* (middle school, junior/senior high reluctant readers). Together, these volumes list thousands of the most recent children's and young adult trade books. Although the works included cover a wide range of topics, they all have one thing in common: they're good books that students and teachers alike enjoy.

Of course, no single book is right for everyone or every purpose, so inclusion in this booklist is not necessarily an endorsement from NCTE. However, it does indicate that the professionals who make up the booklist committee feel that the work in question is worthy of teachers' and students' attention, whether for its informative or aesthetic qualities. On the other hand, exclusion from an NCTE booklist is not necessarily a judgment on the quality of a given book or publisher. Many factors—space, time, availability of certain books, publisher participation—may influence the final shape of the list.

We hope that you will find this booklist a useful resource in discovering new titles and authors, and we hope that you will collect the other booklists in the NCTE series. Our mission is to help improve the teaching and learning of English and the language arts, and we feel the quality of our booklists contributes substantially toward that goal. We think you will agree.

Dawn Boyer
Director of Acquisitions and Development in Publications
National Council of Teachers of English

Contents

Note to the Reader

Reading for pleasure results in both enjoyment and success. Reading brings enjoyment by allowing you to think about new ideas, go places you have never been, consider problems from a different perspective, meet fascinating people, have adventures where you are always the winner, and even live in a different time and place. Reading also brings success in a subtle way; the more you read, the more improvement you will discover in your writing style, spelling, and grammar skills, and in your vocabulary. This success comes with no conscious effort, no assignments or book reports, because just reading what you enjoy will have these results for you. The more you read, the more pleasure and success you will achieve.

A recent survey of teenagers (Mellon 1990) shows they read in their spare time for two main reasons: entertainment and information. One young man said, "I like reading science fiction and mystery, because you never know what's going to happen." Some said reading "takes you to other places . . . helps you to solve problems . . . makes you feel better when you are sad." Others read for information when they are interested in satisfying their curiosity.

Many teenage readers rely on the recommendations of friends when choosing what books to read. In addition to your friends, you can use *High Interest— Easy Reading* as a reference to find good books to read. Here are books, both fiction and nonfiction, published in the years 1993 and 1994. Publishers sent books to our committee, and we selected books of high interest to teen readers. Each book was read by two or more committee members, who then wrote a short annotation describing the book. We have arranged these three hundred titles into nineteen chapters, each indicating a central idea or theme, such as "Adventure," "Dealing with Death," "Sports," and "Science." The chapter titled "Issues of Our Time" includes books that consider such controversial subjects as violence, bigotry, and child abuse. You will also find "Fantasy" and "Mystery," books about famous people, "How-to Books," and many more.

Within each chapter, entries are arranged alphabetically by the author's name (or by title in the few cases of books listing no author) and also include the title, the publisher and year of publication, and the International Standard Book Number (ISBN), to use when ordering a book from the publisher. A brief annotation tells you about the main character and plot, or about the main topic of the book if it is nonfiction. Following each annotation is a listing of any national awards that the book has won. In some cases we suggest companion books you might enjoy if you like a particular book. Where the subject or language is especially mature, we indicate this. At the end of the annotation we also identify *multicultural books* that add to our understanding and appreciation of other cultural traditions, such as African American, Asian American, Hispanic American, and Native American traditions.

At the end of the book are three indexes to help you find the books you want. Find the author you like in the Author Index. If you know only the title, try the Title Index. If you are searching for books on a particular topic—such as Chinese Americans, the Civil War, physical disabilities, space travel and exploration, werewolves—use the Subject Index. Each book in the booklist has been assigned an annotation number; the three indexes list books by this number. A Directory of Publishers lists ordering addresses for all the publishers of books in this volume. We also include an appendix of award-winning books.

Our committee of reviewers has chosen books that we hope you will enjoy reading. If you like a book, say so. Write to the author in care of the publisher's editorial office listed in the Directory of Publishers. Publishers and authors are honored to know how you feel about their work. Include your return address, or perhaps a stamped, self-addressed envelope; you may even receive a reply.

Our goal is to provide a useful reference for you to use in finding books that bring you enjoyment. We know that reading for pleasure also expands your thinking and improves your writing, an added benefit to enjoyment. So choose a topic or an author you like and skim the annotations; then relax and enjoy a new book.

Reference

Mellon, Constance A. 1990. "Leisure Reading Choices of Rural Teens." *School Library Media Quarterly* (Summer): 223–28.

1   Adventure

1.1   Calmenson, Stephanie, adapter. **The Young Indiana Jones Chronicles: Race to Danger.** Random House, 1993. ISBN 0-679-84388-4.

Young Indiana Jones and his girlfriend, Nancy, are high school sweethearts by day and supersleuths by night. When the car that Indy needs for a dance breaks down, he and Nancy go to Thomas Edison's laboratory to get mechanical advice. Instead, they become involved in stolen top-secret plans, a kidnapping, espionage, and an adventure that risks their lives.

1.2   Campbell, Eric. **The Shark Callers.** Harcourt Brace, 1994. ISBN 0-15-200010-0.

When the volcano Matupi erupts off the coast of New Guinea, an island north of Australia, Andy and his family are in the midst of sailing around the world. Suddenly their boat plunges into the whirlpool of a tidal wave. At the same time, Kaleku, a young apprentice hunter learning to become a sacred Shark Caller, also must navigate the tsunami, or tidal wave, in his canoe. This high-pitched adventure novel charts the very different journeys of both young men as they struggle to survive in an ocean teeming with sharks.

1.3   Dunlop, Eileen. **Finn's Search.** Holiday House, 1994. ISBN 0-8234-1099-4.

When a local businessman proposes to develop a gravel pit in their pristine rural neighborhood, Chris and Finn hatch a counterplan. If they can find evidence that their community is built on the site of an ancient Roman fort, then archaeologists will declare the area a historical treasure. The two boys, however, unearth much more than a little dirt; the treasure they discover is an unexpected friendship.

1.4   Martin, Les. **Young Indiana Jones and the Titanic Adventure.** Random House/Bullseye Books, 1993. ISBN 0-679-84925-4.

When Indiana Jones boards the luxurious ocean liner *Titanic,* he is prepared for nothing more than a pleasure cruise. Soon, however, he finds himself enmeshed in a terrifying web of espionage, misguided romance, popular revolution, and a struggle for personal survival. Woven into a tale of youthful adventure are historical and biographical data about Sir Arthur Conan Doyle, the 1916 Irish uprising against Britain, and the sinking of the great ship *Titanic.*

1.5   Martin, Les, adapter. **The Young Indiana Jones Chronicles: Prisoner of War.** Random House, 1993. ISBN 0-679-84389-2.

Young Indiana Jones adopts a new identity in order to receive better treatment from the Germans in a World War II prison camp. Mistakenly identified as a French escape artist, Indy is transferred to a maximum security prison from which no one has ever escaped. Not about to resign himself to captivity, and with his new friend, Charles de Gaulle (based on the French general and president of the same name), Indy devises a bold plan to secure his freedom.

1.6   Paulsen, Gary. **The Car.** Harcourt Brace, 1994. ISBN 0-15-292878-2.

Fourteen-year-old Terry Anderson's parents take off to live their own separate lives, and Terry finds himself at home alone with a Blakely Bearcat car kit. The adventure begins when Terry successfully assembles "the Cat" and heads west to find his uncle. A wandering Vietnam veteran, Waylon Jackson, and his motorcycle-riding buddy, Wayne, become Terry's companions and teachers as they head out "truckin'" across the country, learning about life. Independence from family values may offend some readers.

1.7   Stine, Megan, and H. William Stine. **Young Indiana Jones and the Lost Gold of Durango.** Random House/Bullseye Books, 1993. ISBN 0-679-84926-2.

During a stay in Durango, Colorado, in 1912, Indiana Jones meets up with Jay, a young Pueblo Indian. Jay, whose father was involved in a bank heist with the notorious Butler Brothers, journeys out to the ancient cliff dwellings of Mesa Verde in search of the gold hidden by his father. Indiana joins the adventure, and together they contend with the desert's heat, poisonous snakes, a strange hermit, and the murderous Butler Brothers. Who will discover the gold first?

1.8   Taylor, Theodore. **Timothy of the Cay.** Harcourt Brace, 1993. ISBN 0-15-288358-4.

This story begins where *The Cay* ends. It is 1942, and twelve-year-old Phillip, a white boy just rescued from a remote uncharted Caribbean cay, or island, wonders if he will ever regain his sight in order to return and see the cay for himself. In chapter two, it is 1884, and young Timo-thy, a black boy, looks for work as a cabin boy, filled with hope for a future of sailing the Caribbean. Alternating chapters in this "prequel-sequel" show us how each young man seeks to fulfill his dream, one in the past and one in the present, until their lives intersect. *Multicultural.*

ALA Best Books for Young Adults, 1994
Notable 1994 Children's Trade Books in the Field of Social Studies

2　The Animal World

2.1　Arnold, Caroline. **Dinosaurs All Around: An Artist's View of the Prehistoric World.** Photographs by Richard Hewett. Houghton Mifflin/ Clarion Books, 1993. ISBN 0-395-62363-4.

Caroline Arnold and Richard Hewett document Stephen Czerkas's creative process as a sculptor of life-sized dinosaur models, from sketch to museum-ready exhibit. They reveal a wealth of information about the habitats, physical characteristics, and behaviors of some of the world's most well-researched species of dinosaur.

2.2　Grace, Eric S. **Elephants.** Sierra Club Books for Children, 1993. ISBN 0-87156-538-2.

Elephants are highly intelligent, social, communicative, and enormous creatures. This book in the Sierra Club Wildlife Library series thoroughly investigates the anatomy, behavior patterns, ancestry, and communication systems of modern Asian and African elephants. Close-up color photographs of these animals in their natural habitats and several informative drawings and maps enhance the text. The closing chapter, discussing the relationship between elephants and people, is sure to leave readers with a new interest and concern for this gentle giant.

2.3　Knight, Linsay. **The Sierra Club Book of Small Mammals.** Sierra Club Books for Children, 1993. ISBN 0-87156-525-0.

Did you know that some mammals actually lay eggs and have scales, and that some can fly? There is even a tiny mammal that is related to an elephant. You see, it all started about 195 million years ago. . . . This book has fascinating information about small mammals, with amazing illustrations and photographs.

2.4　Lacey, Elizabeth A. **What's the Difference? A Guide to Some Familiar Animal Look-Alikes.** Illustrated by Robert Shetterly. Houghton Mifflin/Clarion Books, 1993. ISBN 0-395-56182-5.

Was Captain Hook harrassed by a crocodile or an alligator? Should Buffalo Bill's name really have been Bison Bill? Was it a hare and a tortoise who ran the race immortalized by Aesop, or was it actually a rabbit and a turtle? This is the ideal guide for anyone who has ever been confused by look-alike animal pairs. Elizabeth Lacey describes the physical and behavioral features of seven pairs of animals commonly confused with one another, and explains how to distinguish between them.

2.5   Lang, Susan S. **Invisible Bugs and Other Creepy Creatures That Live with You.** Illustrated by Eric C. Lindstrom. Sterling, 1993. ISBN 0-8069-8209-8.

Are bugs bugging you? Did you ever wonder why mosquito bites itch so much? Answer—bug spit. Now you know. Why do mosquitos like some people better than others? Answer—look it up in the section called "Vampire Bugs." What bugs are found in your bed? After reading this book, you will feel like millions of tiny eyes are watching you all the time—that's because they are!

2.6   Maynard, Thane. **Endangered Animal Babies.** Franklin Watts/Cincinnati Zoo Books, 1993. ISBN 0-531-15257-X.

Babies, babies everywhere! All babies are cute, right? Well, here is a collection of babies that need our help. From the air, the land, and the water, all twenty-four of the little ones in this book belong to species that are endangered. Some admittedly have faces and shapes that only a mother could love. The Hyacinth Macaw, for example, begins its life looking very different from the beautiful blue bird of adulthood. What a face! Get involved—we can all help endangered animals.

2.7   Schmidt, Jeremy. **In the Village of the Elephants.** Photographs by Ted Wood. Walker, 1994. ISBN 0-8027-8226-4.

Readers are introduced to a different culture in this large-format book. Using elephants as beasts of burden is a way of life in India. The text, highlighted with clear, full-color photographs, focuses on a father, son, and the elephant with whom they work. There is factual information as well as a description of daily events in the life of Mudumalai, the Indian elephant.

2.8   Taylor, Barbara. **The Bird Atlas.** Illustrated by Richard Orr. Alfred A. Knopf/Dorling Kindersley, 1993. ISBN 1-56458-327-9.

If you are interested in birds, this is the book for you. Here you can read about birds from every continent, from the usual to the unusual. Great photos and drawings fill every page. If you are concerned about the environment, there are suggestions for what you can do to make a difference by helping our feathered friends.

3   Biography

3.1   Aparicio, Frances R., editor. **Latino Voices.** Millbrook Press, 1994. ISBN 1-56294-388-X.

This artful blend of Latino poetry, fiction, and biography examines the history, culture, and social issues of Hispanic Americans. Contemporary Latino writers tell their own stories of family life, faith and hope, language barriers and triumphs, employment, racial discrimination, and the promise of the American dream. The selections in this anthology illustrate the lives and dreams of Hispanic Americans while celebrating cultural pride and individual identity. *Multicultural.*

3.2   Archer, Jules. **They Had a Dream: The Civil Rights Struggle from Frederick Douglass to Marcus Garvey to Martin Luther King and Malcolm X.** Viking, 1993. ISBN 0-670-84494-2.

Though many have contributed to the Civil Rights movement, the work of four men—Frederick Douglass, Marcus Garvey, Martin Luther King Jr., and Malcolm X—stands at the core of the struggle for racial equality. This book in the Epoch Biographies series presents four portraits of courage and determination that will help readers see their own place in the world and discover their own power to change that world. *Multicultural.*

3.3   Bentley, Bill. **Ulysses S. Grant.** Franklin Watts, 1993. ISBN 0-531-20162-7.

Ulysses S. Grant's confidence, determination, and honesty were valuable assets in his military career. Through the use of photographs, illustrations, maps, and lively chapters, this biography provides readers with an overview of Grant's life. We follow him from his early school days in Ohio to his training at West Point, where he wanted to pursue engineering or business. His key role in the Civil War is chronicled, as are his years as the eighteenth president of the United States.

3.4   Cannon, Marion G. **Robert E. Lee.** Franklin Watts, 1993. ISBN 0-531-20120-1.

How could the leader of the losing side in a major war be respected and admired as the best commander in the conflict? General Robert E.

Lee, military leader of the South during the Civil War, is still revered for his military skill and integrity. Even his main opponent, General Ulysses S. Grant, heeded Lee's requests for surrender out of respect for the man. Details of Lee's life as well as significant dates and events of the Civil War are included in this short, easy-to-read volume.

3.5   Cox, Ted. **Mario Lemieux: Super Mario.** Children's Press, 1993. ISBN 0-516-04378-1.

This biography chronicles Mario Lemieux's meteoric rise to fame as a hockey player and MVP for the Pittsburgh Penguins. In addition to his successes on the ice, he must triumph over his greatest obstacle—a type of cancer called Hodgkin's disease. Also featured are impressive action photographs and a chronology of key events in Lemieux's life and career.

3.6   Cox, Ted. **Shaquille O'Neal: Shaq Attack.** Children's Press, 1993. ISBN 0-516-04379-X.

Here is an incredibly large and menacing basketball player—7 ft. 1 in. tall, weighing over 300 pounds—who is quick and can move to either block a shot or dunk a basket. Growing up, he did not take school seriously and got into trouble. Now, as number 32 of the Orlando Magic, Shaq has become one of the greatest centers in the history of basketball. This black basketball star works hard, is friendly and thoughtful, and is loved by the fans. *Multicultural.*

3.7   Dahl, Roald. **My Year.** Viking, 1993. ISBN 0-670-85397-6.

In this stroll through the calendar year, British author and humorist Roald Dahl uses his reflections about the seasons to reveal the universalities of life. His observations about the wildlife and vegetation of the English countryside form a springboard for nostalgic memories of childhood and adolescence that he records here during the final year of his life. *My Year* leaves one with a deeper appreciation for the rhythms of life and a comforting sense of its continuity.

3.8   Freedman, Russell. **Eleanor Roosevelt: A Life of Discovery.** Houghton Mifflin/Clarion Books, 1993. ISBN 0-89919-862-7.

Sprinkled with clear photographs throughout, this biography traces Eleanor Roosevelt's heartache-filled childhood, education, courtship, and eventual marriage to Franklin Delano Roosevelt, who became the thirty-second U.S. president. After FDR's death, she went on to work for universal human rights through the United Nations. Readers will learn how this most unusual woman became one of our most famous first ladies.

ALA Best Books for Young Adults, 1994
ALA Notable Books for Children, 1994
Booklist Editors' Choices, 1993
Boston Globe–Horn Book Nonfiction Award, 1994
Newbery Honor Book, 1994
Notable 1994 Children's Trade Books in the Field of Social Studies
School Library Journal Best Books, 1993

3.9   Gutman, Bill. **Reggie White: Star Defensive Lineman.** Millbrook Press, 1994. ISBN 1-56294-461-4.

Even in his rookie year with the Philadelphia Eagles football team, Reggie White showed that he was a special athlete, with impressive records in tackles and sacks. In college, this African American's first goal was a pro football career, but he had become a minister at the age of seventeen and also was determined to maintain a religious life. His strong belief in God has made White a positive role model, preaching at many churches and working on projects to improve conditions in inner cities. *Multicultural.*

3.10   Heslewood, Juliet. **Introducing Picasso.** Little, Brown, 1993. ISBN 0-316-35917-3.

Introducing Picasso is not merely a biography of renowned artist Pablo Picasso; it is also an excellent guide to art history. Juliet Heslewood explains terms such as *Impressionism, Post-Impressionism, Cubism,* and *avant-garde,* linking them to their historical contexts and to Picasso's work. She introduces Picasso's many mentors and colleagues, detailing their influence on him and his work. A collection of photographs, color reproductions representing Picasso's range of styles, and chart of key dates enhance this readable life story.

3.11   Heyes, Eileen. **Adolf Hitler.** Millbrook Press, 1994. ISBN 1-56294-343-X.

Racism, destruction, violence, and death were all part of everyday life in Adolf Hitler's Germany. How did Germany let itself be led for twelve years by a mass murderer? And why did the world stand by while so many innocents were slaughtered? In one way or another, we have all been affected by the war Hitler started and the crimes he inspired. Eileen Heyes offers facts and photographs in a clear, simple manner, showing frightening similarities between the doctrines of then and now.

3.12   Hoose, Phillip. **It's Our World, Too! Stories of Young People Who Are Making a Difference.** Little, Brown, 1993. ISBN 0-316-37241-2.

You *can* make a difference! These fourteen young people from elementary school through high school did just that. They saw a need and did something about it. Maybe you feel strongly about gang pressure, about saving the dolphins, about world peace, or about racism. Well, don't just sit there, *do* something about it. This book doesn't just tell a story—it gives you the tools you need to make a change. You can do it!

3.13   Krull, Kathleen. **Lives of the Musicians: Good Times, Bad Times (And What the Neighbors Thought).** Illustrated by Kathryn Hewitt. Harcourt Brace, 1993. ISBN 0-15-248010-2.

Which famous Russian composer held onto his head while conducting, for fear that it would fall off? Which English lyricist was kidnapped and held for ransom in Italy when he was two years old? Which French musician owned 200 umbrellas but no bed? In this masterpiece of research, Kathleen Krull presents short biographies of twenty of the world's greatest musical geniuses, examining both the professional accomplishments and the personal eccentricities that make these musicians such fascinating people.

Boston Globe–Horn Book Nonfiction Honor Book, 1993

3.14   Lewin, Ted. **I Was a Teenage Professional Wrestler.** Orchard Books, 1993. ISBN 0-531-05477-2.

In words and pictures, here is the story of illustrator Ted Lewin's years as an art student at Brooklyn's Pratt Institute, where he paid for his studies by wrestling professionally at night. His knowledge of and affection for the wrestling life is apparent on every page: "It was a great life, crowded with unforgettable characters: college men, working men, ugly men, huge fat men in outrageous costumes, men from all over the world." A companion novel to this most unusual autobiography is Robert Lipsyte's *The Chief* (18.10).

3.15   Lipsyte, Robert. **Arnold Schwarzenegger: Hercules in America.** HarperCollins, 1993. ISBN 0-06-023002-9.

After growing up in post–World War II Austria, Arnold Schwarzenegger came to America to start a new life. The story of this world champion bodybuilder encourages physical fitness and perseverance, detailing his failures and successes as his career moved from physical prowess to Hollywood and politics. A book in the Superstar Lineup series. *Multicultural.*

3.16   Lipsyte, Robert. **Jim Thorpe: Twentieth-Century Jock.** HarperCollins, 1993. ISBN 0-06-022988-8.

Jim Thorpe, stripped of his Native American languages and customs and drilled in the ways of whites, became one of America's greatest all-around athletes. On his father's side, Thorpe was a descendant of Black Hawk, chief of the Sac and Fox Nation, and his maternal grandmother was a Potawatomie; other grandparents were of Irish and French descent. Thorpe went on to become an Olympic medal winner in track and field in 1912 and later a professional football and baseball player. He was a "spirit of his time, a symbol of a country flexing its muscles in the world arena, a person who would not be beaten down." Thorpe's story is a chronicle of the American spirit as well as American sport. A book in the Superstar Lineup series. *Multicultural.*

3.17   Lipsyte, Robert. **Joe Louis: A Champ for All America.** HarperCollins/ Harper Trophy Books, 1994. ISBN 0-06-446155-6.

Until recently, racial discrimination prevented outstanding black men and women from competing in national sports. Joe Louis, the "Brown Bomber," was one of the first athletes to break down barriers of prejudice in America. Here is the story of his rise to boxing fame as world heavyweight champion from 1937 to 1949. During his career he lost only three of seventy-one bouts, but he paid a high personal price to become the inspiration for athletes of all races. Numerous photos add further detail to the heart-lifting story of this superhero. A book in the Superstar Lineup series. *Multicultural.*

3.18   Lipsyte, Robert. **Michael Jordan: A Life above the Rim.** HarperCollins, 1994. ISBN 0-06-024235-3.

Robert Lipsyte describes the three elements in Michael Jordan's life that produced his rise to legendary stature as a basketball player—his family life, his persistent personality, and his athletic prowess. Lipsyte balances this portrayal of Jordan as sports superhero, however, with remarks about the African American player's sadder side, citing his gambling addiction and the tragic murder of his father. A book in the Superstar Lineup series. *Multicultural.*

3.19   Littlefield, Bill. **Champions: Stories of Ten Remarkable Athletes.** Illustrated by Bernie Fuchs. Little, Brown, 1993. ISBN 0-316-52805-6.

Stories of ten champions in different sports reveal both the heroism and the ordinariness of these athletes' lives. Accounts of the struggles and successes of such celebrities as tennis great Billie Jean King and soccer superstar Pelé are not just about physical challenge. They demonstrate a triumph of the human spirit over the many political and social obstacles standing in the way of female, minority, and physically challenged competitors. *Multicultural.*

3.20 Macnow, Glen. **David Robinson: Star Center.** Enslow, 1994. ISBN 0-89490-483-3.

In just a few short years, David Robinson has become one of the brightest stars in pro basketball. From his college days at the U.S. Naval Academy to his participation on the U.S. Olympic "Dream Team," Robinson has played a stunning game. But basketball is not the only interest for this black superstar. Find out more about David Robinson the man in this exciting biography. *Multicultural.*

3.21 Rappoport, Ken. **Shaquille O'Neal.** Walker, 1994. ISBN 0-8027-8294-9.

This lively compilation of interviews, news articles, family anecdotes, and personal history traces the life story of African American superstar Shaquille O'Neal. From his childhood days as an "army brat" to his Louisiana State University college days and his selection as the number one draft pick by the Orlando Magic, the reader grows to respect O'Neal's talent and determination in this portrait of one basketball player's rise to NBA fame. *Multicultural.*

3.22 Reiser, Howard. **Barry Sanders: Lion with a Quiet Roar.** Children's Press, 1993. ISBN 0-516-04377-3.

Many consider Barry Sanders the best running back in professional football, yet he has always remained humble, even shy, and respectful of others. This African American player demonstrates that success in sports is never earned without sustained, disciplined effort. Highlighted are Sanders's childhood, college days, and professional career with the Detroit Lions, where he models team spirit and personal integrity. A book in the Sports Stars series. *Multicultural.*

3.23 Ryan, Cary, editor. **Louisa May Alcott: Her Girlhood Diary.** Troll Associates/Bridgewater Books, 1993. ISBN 0-8167-3140-3.

Little of Louisa May Alcott's girlhood diary has survived—much of it was destroyed by Alcott herself before her death. What Cary Ryan has done in this book is take Alcott's diary entries, letters, and poems exactly as they were written when she was a young girl between the ages of ten and fourteen and combine these with a narrative about the famous author's life. Alcott's lively spirit and quiet genius shine through even her earliest scribblings, giving us insight into the characters in her books and into her own life.

3.24   Sandak, Cass R. **The Reagans.** Crestwood House, 1993. ISBN 0-89686-646-7.

In this behind-the-scenes look into the lives of one American president and his family, readers learn how Ronald Reagan struggled in his early years and got his start in show business. He became president of the Screen Actors Guild, and that led him into politics. Reagan was elected governor of California in 1966 and president of the United States in 1980. The book also describes Reagan's family life and introduces readers to First Lady Nancy Reagan.

3.25   Sandak, Cass R. **The Tafts.** Crestwood House, 1993. ISBN 0-89686-647-5.

Old black-and-white photos bring the times of William Taft to life. From his birth to death (1857–1930), his interesting childhood and career are chronicled in this factual but warm volume. Taft was pushed to the White House by his wife, Nellie, where his dislike of hurting anyone's feelings kept him from making decisions. Taft loved his family and had a great sense of humor. He is more admired for his tenure as chief justice of the Supreme Court than as president. This fast-moving, engaging book packed with historical information is for readers interested in learning more about early twentieth century presidents and first ladies.

3.26   Sanford, William R., and Carl R. Green. **Kareem Abdul-Jabbar.** Crestwood House, 1993. ISBN 0-89686-737-4.

Kareem Abdul-Jabbar proved his ability on the basketball court as a rookie and continued to demonstrate his prowess at the end of his career, when he was the oldest NBA player on the courts. A black raised in a predominantly white environment, Abdul-Jabbar grew up knowing the importance of an education. Trivia questions are scattered throughout the book to present more facts about this shy, engaging man and his incredible athletic career. *Multicultural.*

3.27   Sanford, William R., and Carl R. Green. **Muhammad Ali.** Crestwood House, 1993. ISBN 0-89686-739-0.

"I am the greatest!" Muhammad Ali made this phrase famous. Would you believe a skinny twelve-year-old black boy named Cassius Clay could become a superstar? He didn't believe it either, at first. He started to think about fighting when his bike was stolen. That was the beginning of his remarkable boxing career. He fought more than just his opponent in the ring and triumphed. This biography includes a Muhammad Ali trivia quiz and some suggestions for additional reading if you enjoy the world of boxing. *Multicultural.*

3.28 Simon, Charnan. **Midori: Brilliant Violinist.** Children's Press, 1993. ISBN 0-516-04187-8.

Japanese-born Mi Dori Goto is a musical genius who began her music training at the age of three and her professional career as a concert violinist at the age of fourteen. The book tells of her years as a student, her development as a professional in the United States, and the sacrifices and rewards of discipline. Midori is a wonderful example of a young person whose passion for her art takes her to unprecedented heights. *Multicultural.*

3.29 Sinnott, Susan. **Extraordinary Asian Pacific Americans.** Children's Press, 1993. ISBN 0-516-03052-X.

For centuries, Asian Pacific people have played a major role in the founding and growth of America. Through the eyes of the participants, experience the Asian Pacific immigration to America. Watch the gold miners, the Chinese railroad workers, or the prisoners of Angel Island. Share the experiences of inmates in America's World War II detention camps. Eighty-three biographical sketches include novelist Amy Tan, anchorwoman Connie Chung, scholar and politician S. I. Hayakawa, and martial arts expert Bruce Lee. *Multicultural.*

3.30 Slater, Jack. **Malcolm X.** Children's Press, 1993. ISBN 0-516-06669-2.

Having suffered a childhood of poverty, racism, and violence, Malcolm Little found himself in prison at the age of twenty. He began studying the teachings of the Nation of Islam, finally converting to the religion of Islam. He became the Black Muslim Malcolm X, working to foster self-respect among all African Americans. His message differed from that of other black leaders in the Civil Rights movement; he felt that violence was justified for the self-protection of black people. A book in the Cornerstones of Freedom series. *Multicultural.*

3.31 Sullivan, George. **Mathew Brady: His Life and Photographs.** Dutton/Cobblehill Books, 1994. ISBN 0-525-65186-1.

Mathew Brady's photographs of Civil War battles and casualties shocked his viewers, forcing them to acknowledge the brutal reality of war. Brady, recognizing the value of a visual record of people and events, photographed most of the prominent people of his time. Photographs of both Brady and many of his most famous subjects are included here.

3.32   Sullivan, Michael T. **Top 10 Baseball Pitchers.** Enslow, 1994. ISBN 0-89490-520-1.

This volume in the Sports Top Ten series selects ten top athletes from the sport of baseball and presents short summaries of each player's professional accomplishments. Black-and-white and color photographs of the players enhance the text. A listing of birthdates, colleges, pro teams played for, records, and honors provides a quick summary of each athlete's career. Other books in the series feature the top players in basketball, football, and hockey. *Multicultural.*

3.33   Turner, Robyn Montana. **Frida Kahlo.** Little, Brown, 1993. ISBN 0-316-85651-7.

Frida Kahlo is a famous Mexican artist with a lust for life. Seriously injured in a bus accident, the bedridden youngster took up painting to amuse herself. Years later, she became Mexico's foremost female artist and the wife of muralist Diego Rivera. This biography in the Portraits of Women Artists for Children series includes several photographs of Kahlo and her family and many color reproductions of her artwork. Her surreal self-portraits hauntingly reflect the contrasting feelings of pain and hope that characterize her life. *Multicultural.*

3.34   van der Rol, Ruud, and Rian Verhoeven (translated by Tony Langham and Plym Peters). **Anne Frank: Beyond the Diary.** Viking, 1993. ISBN 0-670-84932-4.

Photographs, illustrations, and maps accompany historical essays, diary excerpts, and interviews in this extraordinary window to the world of Anne Frank and the massive upheaval that tore her world apart. For the first time, Anne's life before her family went into hiding in Amsterdam from the Nazis is revealed, as well as influences that formed her strong moral beliefs. Included are over 100 photographs taken by Anne Frank's father and others.

ALA Best Books for Young Adults, 1994
ALA Notable Books for Children, 1994
ALA Quick Picks for Young Adults, 1994
Booklist Editors' Choices, 1993
IRA Teachers' Choices, 1994
Notable 1994 Children's Trade Books in the Field of Social Studies
School Library Journal Best Books, 1993

3.35   Venezia, Mike. **Georgia O'Keeffe.** Children's Press, 1993. ISBN 0-516-02297-0.

At a time when women painters were not taken seriously, Georgia O'Keeffe (1887–1986) boldly set forth to explore, develop, and realize her talent as a painter. From her childhood on a farm in Wisconsin to New York and, finally, New Mexico, O'Keeffe captured on canvas the beauty of natural objects by using bold colors, clear lines, and larger-than-life perspective in her own unique style. The large, clear text and beautiful color reproductions in this book in the Getting to Know the World's Greatest Artists series bring O'Keeffe's life and work to young readers.

3.36   Yannuzzi, Della A. **Wilma Mankiller: Leader of the Cherokee Nation.** Enslow, 1994. ISBN 0-89490-498-1.

At the age of twelve, Wilma Mankiller experienced the first of many difficult transitions in her young life: her Cherokee family moved from their Oklahoma farm to an apartment in San Francisco. Overnight, Mankiller had to adjust not only to urban life but to life in a culture that often perceived her cherished Native American heritage as alien and comic. Mankiller ultimately graduated from college and, in 1985, was the first female to become principal chief of the Cherokee Nation, remaining a forceful leader of her people today. *Multicultural.*

4 Dealing with Death

4.1   Conly, Jane Leslie. **Crazy Lady!** HarperCollins/Laura Geringer Books, 1993. ISBN 0-06-021357-4.

When Vernon's mom dies, his grades fall lower than ever. He and his friends make fun of the "crazy lady" who walks in the middle of the street with her mentally disabled son. Vernon's tutor, elderly Miss Annie, helps him bring up his grades, and he helps the "crazy lady" as she struggles to raise her son and fight alcoholism. Vernon learns there are many ways to be "smart."

Newbery Honor Book, 1994

4.2   Creech, Sharon. **Walk Two Moons.** HarperCollins, 1994. ISBN 0-06-023334-6.

Salamanca Tree Hiddle, who is of Seneca Indian ancestry, is traveling from Ohio to Idaho with her eccentric grandparents. Along the way, she tells them the "extensively strange" story of Phoebe Winterbottom, her disappearing mother, and the lunatic. Beneath this story is Sal's pilgrimage to find her own mother and bring her back home. The story is mysterious, funny, and charming, with the most lovable characters you will meet. *Multicultural.*

Newbery Medal, 1995

4.3   Deaver, Julie Reece. **You Bet Your Life.** HarperCollins/Charlotte Zolotow Books, 1993. ISBN 0-06-021516-X.

Seventeen-year-old Bess, who wants to be able to make people laugh, works as an intern on a popular television comedy show. Her positive sense of humor helps her come to terms with the suicide of her mother and deal with her distraught father. Bess meets Elliot, the elevator operator at work. Together they form a comedy team and plan to try out some of her material at a comedy club, with surprising results.

4.4   Eskridge, Ann E. **The Sanctuary.** Dutton/Cobblehill Books, 1994. ISBN 0-525-65168-3.

Little Man meets old Mrs. Johnson—that is, she catches him. Everyone says she is a witch. She has a yard full of junk but insists that it is really a "sanctuary" for the dead: a place where their spirits can be put to rest. Maybe this old woman can finally help Little Man deal with the senseless death of his own father. But first, he must save that sanctuary from being torn down by the neighborhood.

4.5 Garland, Sherry. **The Silent Storm.** Harcourt Brace, 1993. ISBN 0-15-274170-4.

Alyssa loved the power of hurricanes and stories about storms at sea until a real hurricane hit Galveston Island, killing both her parents. Overcome by grief, Alyssa has not spoken in the three years since her parents' death. Now, as she battles yet another hurricane in her coastal Texas community, Alyssa searches for her voice and her memories of that earlier storm. Aided by her grandfather, Alyssa discovers connections she never expected to find between herself and the rest of her family. A similar story is Gloria Whelan's *A Time to Keep Silent* (4.12).

4.6 Goodman, Joan Elizabeth. **Songs from Home.** Harcourt Brace, 1994. ISBN 0-15-203591-5.

How about singing in the streets of Rome for your dinner? This is what young Anna does while attempting to find out more about her family in America and about her deceased mother, subjects her father avoids. If that is not bad enough, they live in a dilapidated boarding house, and Anna must put up with being the "odd duck" American at an Italian school. Adult decisions face both father and daughter when a vacationing family member from Missouri recognizes them. The story culminates in a powerful ending.

4.7 Greene, Constance C. **Nora: Maybe a Ghost Story.** Harcourt Brace/Browndeer Press, 1993. ISBN 0-15-276895-5.

Influenced by the memory of their recently deceased mother, Nora and Patsy try to sabotage their lonely father's new romance with "The Tooth." They must also cope with an aging, flamboyant grandmother. Threatening the girls' relationship is the fact that they both have a crush on the same boy. The two sisters use different tactics as they struggle to survive a trying time.

4.8 Jenkins, Lyll Becerra de. **Celebrating the Hero.** Dutton/Lodestar Books, 1993. ISBN 0-525-67399-7.

After the death of her mother, Camila Draper travels from her home in Connecticut to her mother's hometown of San Javier, Colombia, to attend a special ceremony honoring her grandfather, Francisco Zamora. In her quest to understand her mother's past, Camila uncovers troubling family secrets and learns the truth about her illustrious grandfather. Through this journey, Camila comes to understand her family as well as the complex relationship between love and forgiveness. *Multicultural.*

4.9   Johnson, Angela. **Toning the Sweep.** Orchard Books, 1993. ISBN 0-531-05476-4.

How do you live with pain in its many forms? Three remarkable black women—Grandmama Ola, her daughter Diane, and her granddaughter Emmie—do so by laughing and celebrating each moment of life. This story, filled with love and laughter set against shadowy, stark death and prejudice, leaves readers with a sense of goodness in life and hope for the future. Emmie gains a new understanding of her family's history and herself from her terminally ill grandmother. *Multicultural.*

Coretta Scott King Award for Writing, 1994

4.10   Peck, Robert Newton. **A Part of the Sky.** Alfred A. Knopf/Borzoi Books, 1994. ISBN 0-679-43277-9.

At the death of his father, thirteen-year-old Robert is forced into adulthood. His struggles to pay the $12 monthly farm payments are complicated by the death of his ox, a drought that takes his crop, and the bank's repossessing the farm on which his father is buried. In this memorable sequel to *A Day No Pigs Would Die,* Robert attempts to balance the challenges of pitiful wages and little sleep as he attends school and courts a girl.

4.11   Springer, Nancy. **Toughing It.** Harcourt Brace, 1994. ISBN 0-15-200011-9.

A rifle explodes and the dirt bike careens, dumping Tuff and Dillon. Dillon is dead, shot in the neck. Enraged and devastated, Tuff leaves the dirty trailer and his drunken mother, doggedly risking his own life to find his brother's killer. Mature situations and blunt language are appropriate to the tension and neglect in Tuff's life of too little love.

Edgar Allan Poe/Mystery Writers of America Award for Best Young Adult Novel, 1995

4.12   Whelan, Gloria. **A Time to Keep Silent.** William B. Eerdmans, 1993. ISBN 0-8028-0118-8.

After her mother's death, Clair Lothrop battles against the frightening changes in her life by refusing to speak. She and her father begin a new life in the country, where Clair meets a unique new friend, Dorrie.

Together they rummage through local junk yards in search of construction materials for an addition to Dorrie's hideaway. Dorrie helps Clair learn to care and feel again, to see a new perspective on what has real value in life. A similar story is Sherry Garland's *The Silent Storm* (4.5).

5   Family Life

5.1   Auch, Mary Jane. **The Latchkey Dog.** Little, Brown, 1994. ISBN 0-316-05916-1.

When his neighbor complains about the disturbance, young Sam must find a way to control his dog, Amber, while the family is away from the house during the day. After unsuccessful attempts to readjust Amber's biological clock, counteract the dog's loneliness with a blaring television, and provide a feline role model, Sam finally finds a solution that works. In the process, he and Amber touch the lives of many in a delightful way.

5.2   Bergman, Ingmar (translated by Joan Tate). **Sunday's Children.** Little, Brown/Arcade Books, 1993. ISBN 1-55970-244-3.

Children born on Sundays are supposed to be special, possessing such gifts as imagination, sensitivity, and the ability to see ghosts. This story recounts the summer vacation of Pu, an eight-year-old boy who experiences the joys and misfortunes of a large Swedish family at the turn of the century. As a sensitive youth, Pu reflects not only on his parents' difficult marriage but also on his growing isolation from the father he worships.

5.3   Bontemps, Arna, and Langston Hughes. **Popo and Fifina.** Illustrated by E. Simms Campbell. Oxford University Press, 1993. ISBN 0-19-508765-8.

Popo and Fifina live on the island of Haiti in the 1930s. When their family moves from its rural mountain home to a village by the sea, readers share the excitement of life's everyday adventures from young Popo's perspective. Gathering water, flying a kite, listening to the night drums fill the air, going fishing, and working in Uncle Jacques's carpentry shop all speak to the mystery and joy of childhood in the simple, yet rich, poetic language of Arna Bontemps and Langston Hughes. Originally published in 1932. *Multicultural.*

5.4   Deem, James M. **Three NBs of Julian Drew.** Houghton Mifflin, 1994. ISBN 0-395-69453-1.

Lonely and severely mentally disturbed, Julian Drew begins an odyssey of self-discovery when he purchases his first NB (notebook) and begins to reveal his despair by writing in code about life with his physically and emotionally abusive stepmother and father. Julian runs away, attempting to re-create a happier past life before his mother died. Susan, a girl from Julian's class who has become his friend, joins him, and together they struggle to find some hope in their desperate situation. This is difficult reading with part of the text written in Julian's code. Mature situations with raw emotional impact may disturb some readers.

5.5   Duffey, Betsy. **Coaster.** Viking, 1994. ISBN 0-670-85480-8.

Twelve-year-old Hart grapples with the problems of his parents' divorce, an irresponsible dad he idolizes, and his mother's new nerdy boyfriend, local weatherman Dub Dugan. Hart's love of roller coasters takes him up and down in his personal ride toward self-understanding and maturity.

5.6   Farmer, Nancy. **Do You Know Me?** Illustrated by Shelley Jackson. Orchard Books, 1993. ISBN 0-531-05474-8.

"Crazy" Uncle Zeka comes to live with his family in Zimbabwe. He takes Tapiwa, his niece, with him on his many misadventures and becomes her close friend. While the setting is contemporary Africa, readers discover that even in a different culture, relatives can be hard to handle. *Multicultural.*

5.7   Feiffer, Jules. **The Man in the Ceiling.** HarperCollins, 1993. ISBN 0-06-205035-4.

Jimmy Jibbett is no good at sports and not much better in school, but he can draw. That is what he does just about every minute of the day. Jimmy's father thinks he is wasting his time dreaming about becoming a great cartoonist. So does everyone else until Charley Beemer, Montclair's best preteen athlete, decides Jimmy has talent. The two team up to create comics together, and a new superhero, Mini-Man, is born.

5.8   Jones, Robin D. **The Beginning of Unbelief.** Atheneum, 1993. ISBN 0-689-31781-6.

Hal does not fit in anywhere—with his divorced parents, his younger sister, or his classmates. In fact, his best friend and confidant is Zach, a voice in Hal's head who also becomes the main character in Hal's science fiction story. This novel not only charts Hal's personal quest for identity but also chronicles Zach's journey through the galaxies. In the process of writing these adventures, Hal discovers a whole new dimension to his own personality.

5.9   Kimmel, Eric A. **One Good Tern Deserves Another.** Holiday House, 1994. ISBN 0-8234-1138-9.

After his stepfather's death, fourteen-year-old Peebee Floyd and his mom move from Oklahoma to the Oregon coast. Here he meets the girl of his dreams, Lani, who introduces him to the wildlife along the coast. Together they discover romance and sunken treasure. However, Peebee is uncomfortable when his mom begins to show a romantic interest in Lani's dad.

5.10   Mango, Karin N. **Portrait of Miranda.** HarperCollins/Charlotte Zolotow Books, 1993. ISBN 0-06-021777-4.

Miranda is haunted by her deceased grandmother. Whenever she walks by her grandmother's portrait, the eyes seem to follow her. Though Miranda resembles her grandmother, she feels she can never be anything like this vibrant woman. Miranda's involvement with a homeless woman helps her learn about her ancestors and her family as she discovers herself.

5.11   Marino, Jan. **For the Love of Pete.** Little, Brown, 1993. ISBN 0-316-54627-5.

After living with Gram all of her life, Phoebe's world turns upside down when her grandmother has to move into a nursing home. In company with Gram's butler and chauffeur, Phoebe begins a journey to Maine, seeking the father she has never known. They encounter a multitude of problems, including Phoebe's unwillingness to leave her grandmother and apprehensions about meeting her father.

5.12   Perkins, Mitali. **The Sunita Experiment.** Little, Brown, 1993. ISBN 0-316-69943-8.

Sunita's grandparents are coming—not for a weekend visit, but for a whole year. They are from India and are very old-fashioned. This is the situation thirteen-year-old Sunita finds herself in, just when school and life are so good, and her romance with Michael Morrison is progressing so nicely. Now, no more boys are allowed in the house, and pizza is a thing of the past as Sunita faces her Indian heritage. *Multicultural.*

5.13   Roybal, Laura. **Billy.** Houghton Mifflin, 1994. ISBN 0-395-67649-5.

Is his name Billy or Will? Does he call New Mexico or Iowa home? Is his father Guillermo Melendez or Dave Campbell? A young Hispanic American boy struggles to sort out his dual identity in this novel. At age ten, Will is kidnapped by his biological father. He becomes Billy, moves to New Mexico, and lives a dramatically different life on the rodeo circuit. When Billy is sixteen, he is located by his adoptive father and sent north to Iowa to return to his former life and family. *Billy* raises some intriguing questions about the adjustments that a child with two families and two pasts must make. *Multicultural.*

5.14   Sharmat, Mitchell. **Hello . . . This Is My Father Speaking.** HarperCollins, 1994. ISBN 0-06-024469-0.

Jeff Whitty is mortified when his father masquerades around town as Mr. Sanitary Master, the mascot for his janitorial business. When Jeff becomes interested in the workings of the stock market, he devises a plan to make his father rich so that he can give up the embarrassing business. Plans go awry, however, and Jeff is more humiliated than ever when 30,000 bushels of wheat are about to be deposited on his father's front lawn.

6 Fantasy

6.1 Banks, Lynne Reid. **The Mystery of the Cupboard.** Morrow Junior Books, 1993. ISBN 0-688-12138-1.

When Omri's family moves to a country house that his mother has inherited from a long-lost cousin, Omri uncovers an ancient sealed cashbox and journal written by his great-great-aunt. Compelled to open the magic cupboard again, he encounters more little people attempting to use him to change the past. Omri discovers the link between this house and the magic cupboard, and he faces the consequences of his choice. Sequel to *The Indian in the Cupboard, The Return of the Indian,* and *The Secret of the Indian.*

6.2 Black, J. R. **The Ghost of Chicken Liver Hill.** Random House/Bullseye Books, 1993. ISBN 0-679-85007-4.

Toby Bemus has always been the class nerd, never acting up or breaking a rule, until he encounters a local ghost. Before long he is cutting class, breaking and entering, and alienating his best friend, all under the guardianship of Buddy Parker, a ghost who is determined to clear up some of the rumors relating to his death. In the process of aiding Buddy, Toby discovers some fascinating history about the police chief and his wife, his homeroom teacher, and even his own mother. A book in the Shadow Zone series.

6.3 Black, J. R. **Guess Who's Dating a Werewolf?** Random House/Bullseye Books, 1993. ISBN 0-679-85008-2.

When Annie Dubinski develops her first crush, it is on her sister's boyfriend, Jake Woolverton. But Jake looks different in the moonlight: fangs, claws, and the killer instinct of a wild animal. "He smiled slowly, and we watched in horror as his sparkling teeth grew into the sharp, pointed fangs of a wolf!" Can Annie save her sister before it is too late? Can she help Jake? A book in the Shadow Zone series.

6.4 Black, J. R. **The Witches Next Door.** Random House/Bullseye Books, 1993. ISBN 0-679-85108-9.

Have you ever wondered what it is like to be a witch? Have you ever met a *real* witch? The two Nightingale sisters, Emma and Abigail, are seemingly harmless old ladies who live next door to Jennifer. She and her friends become curious about the sisters and their increasingly mysterious, playful "tricks." Jennifer, frightened and annoyed at these tricks, gradually involves herself in a series of adventures with the Nightingales. Soon she discovers her own amazing powers. A book in the Shadow Zone series.

6.5 Charnas, Suzy McKee. **The Kingdom of Kevin Malone.** Harcourt Brace/Jane Yolen Books, 1993. ISBN 0-15-200756-3.

Amy is skating in Central Park, minding her own business as she tries to get over the sudden death of Aunt Shelly. Then Kevin Malone, a bully from the past, skates up and slaps a pin onto Amy's sweater—a pin he stole from her when she was a little girl. The chase is on. Except one minute Kevin is there, and the next he has vanished. Amy follows and finds herself in a fantasy world that is not entirely pleasant.

6.6 Heintze, Ty. **Valley of the Eels.** Illustrated by Ty Heintze. Eakin Press, 1993. ISBN 0-89015-904-1.

What a great day! Vacation is on the way, and Shawn seems to have developed a relationship with a dolphin he has named Cloud. Did he just hear Cloud say, "friend"? Cloud leads Shawn and his friend Billy to an underwater dome where they meet Lanor, a boy from the planet Lios. Meanwhile, they stumble across what looks suspiciously like an illegal toxic waste dump.

6.7 Jordan, Sherryl. **Wolf-Woman.** Houghton Mifflin, 1994. ISBN 0-395-70932-6.

At the age of three, Tanith is taken from a den of wolves to live with a clan of savage hunters. As she grows older, she reestablishes her close, intuitive harmony with the wolves, the forest, and the ways of the wild. Ridiculed and eventually shunned by her clan, Tanith must make the ultimate decision: life with the hunters, or life as a wise woman who runs with the wolves.

6.8 Koller, Jackie French. **A Dragon in the Family.** Illustrated by Judith Mitchell. Little, Brown, 1993. ISBN 0-316-50151-4.

When Darek adopts a baby dragon as his pet, he challenges his society's most fundamental precept—that dragons are the enemy. Darek becomes a leader who must expose the mistaken ideas to which his people cling, even though his family is endangered by his courageous stance.

6.9   Levy, Robert. **Clan of the Shape-Changers.** Houghton Mifflin, 1994. ISBN 0-395-66612-0.

Imagine a society where green eyes are a mark of sorcery, where anyone who bears this mark is suspected of witchcraft. The gift of shape-changing is given to very few, but the rulers of Enstor are threatened by it and are determined to exterminate anyone blessed or cursed with such a mark. Susan and a young boy find themselves caught in the middle of a fight for power and control of their world.

6.10   Levy, Robert. **Escape from Exile.** Houghton Mifflin, 1993. ISBN 0-395-64379-1.

Surrounded by talking snakes, green dogs, and other creatures he does not recognize, Daniel realizes he is no longer on Earth. He has landed in Lithia, a place torn apart by bitter civil war and feuding rulers, where he must choose which side to support. When he discovers he can communicate telepathically with animals, they band together to find peace for their land and a way back home for Daniel.

6.11   Pierce, Richard. **The Creation.** Berkley, 1994. ISBN 0-425-14361-9.

Sara Watkins and Josh Frank are in love. However, when Josh traces his family line back to Victor Frankenstein, he is horrified at the evil he discovers, and he commits suicide. Sara, refusing to accept Josh's death, vows to bring Josh back to life and, in doing so, discovers herself in a predicament similar to that of the original Dr. Frankenstein. Can she live with the Josh that she has brought back from the dead? Book one of the Frankenstein's Children series.

6.12   Scott, Michael. **Gemini Game.** Holiday House, 1993. ISBN 0-8234-1092-7.

It is the twenty-first century. Liz and BJ, fifteen-year-old twins, are wealthy, respected computer game designers on Earth until they learn that twelve players of Night's Castle have become comatose while playing the popular virtual reality game. Will fugitives Liz and BJ be able to find a copy of their game in the environmental ruins of the twentieth century? They must find and kill the computer virus in order to restore their freedom and heal the stricken players.

6.13   Shetterly, Will. **NeverNever.** Harcourt Brace/Jane Yolen Books, 1993. ISBN 0-15-257022-5.

Talk about a bad day. Ron manages to annoy a faerie, and suddenly he is changed into Wolfboy. He discovers there are some positive things about the change: his sense of smell is great; he can run faster than anything; and he intimidates most of the other residents of Bordertown, something that is not easy to do. Magic is the name of the game here, and payback is the order of the day in this sequel to *Elsewhere.*

6.14   Sleator, William. **Others See Us.** Dutton Children's Books, 1993. ISBN 0-525-45104-8.

Jared's summer vacation at the family compound catapults from the familiar to the bizarre. When the brakes on his bike fail, he falls into a toxic swamp. The chemicals cause strange changes in his brain; suddenly he can read others' minds. After Jared discovers Grandma also has these controlling powers, the story weaves through mystery and lurking evil.

6.15   Smith, Sherwood. **Wren's Quest.** Harcourt Brace/Jane Yolen Books, 1993. ISBN 0-15-200976-0.

People just don't seem to keep the same shape for two minutes in this sequel to *Wren to the Rescue.* Wren and Prince Connor have both dabbled in magic, but nothing like this. All of a sudden they both become Fish People and are running for their lives. Wren said she wanted adventure, but she gets a bit more than she expected when she sets off on a quest to find her birth parents.

6.16   Wrede, Patricia C. **Calling on Dragons.** Harcourt Brace/Jane Yolen Books, 1993. ISBN 0-15-200950-7.

Morwen is not an ordinary witch; she is a young, pretty witch with nine cats that talk and with lilacs in her garden, along with the required poison oak and wolfsbane. Dastardly wizards have stolen a magic sword that threatens the Enchanted Forest where she lives. In the company of the lovely young queen, a dragon, a six-foot blue donkey, and others, Morwen is off to save the day.

6.17   Zambreno, Mary Frances. **Journeyman Wizard.** Harcourt Brace/Jane Yolen Books, 1994. ISBN 0-15-200022-4.

In this sequel to *A Plague of Sorcerers,* Jermyn Graves continues his studies in the art of sorcery by becoming a student to a famous spellmaker, Lady Jean Allons. He travels to Land's End with his "familiar," a skunk named Delia who aids him in performing magic. There Jermyn must solve many mysteries, not the least of which is discovering the identity of the true killer of Lady Jean, a crime for which he himself is imprisoned.

6.18   Zindel, Paul. **Loch.** HarperCollins Children's Books, 1994. ISBN 0-
06-024542-5.

Fifteen-year-old Loch and his younger sister join their father aboard a
high-tech yacht designed for tracking unexplained phenomena sighted
in a Vermont lake. When a monster explodes from the deep, Loch
finds he must play a deadly game to save those he loves from these
killers. At the same time, he must fight to protect the remarkable creatures from being destroyed forever, without becoming their dinner himself.

7   Folklore and Legends

7.1   Baumann, Kurt (translated and adapted by Naomi Lewis). **The Hungry One.** Illustrated by Stasys Eidrigevičius. North-South Books, 1993. ISBN 1-55858-121-9.

Strange is the tale of "Rum Tum Tum,/ Who felt so empty and so glum/ He'd eat a field and all things in it,/ Then look for more in half a minute./ Feared by all and loved by none,/ He was called the Hungry One." So begins the ballad of Rum Tum Tum. This haunting book, with its lyrical poem and mysterious pictures, has the raw power of a classic fairy tale.

7.2   Fine, Anne. **The Chicken Gave It to Me.** Illustrated by Cynthia Fisher. Little, Brown, 1993. ISBN 0-316-28316-9.

Gemma, a small but determined chicken, sets out to spread the word about the deplorable treatment of her species and others. "Call me chicken no longer! For I had decided upon a plan so bold, so daring, so foolhardy, I frankly doubted if anyone, anywhere, would ever truly think of me as a chicken again." Delightfully illustrated, this story will make you both laugh and think. A drumstick will never look the same again.

7.3   Fox, Paula. **Amzat and His Brothers.** Illustrated by Emily Arnold McCully. Orchard Books, 1993. ISBN 0-531-05462-4.

Paula Fox retells three Italian folktales passed on to her by a friend whose grandfather told him the tales when he was a child. A thread of dark humor runs through the tales, making them inappropriate for small children; however, their common theme of the underdog who prevails against injustice is appealing to an older audience. Figs, terra-cotta pots, olive groves, and other Italian curiosities contribute a strong element of cultural authenticity to the stories. *Multicultural.*

7.4   Lester, Julius. **The Last Tales of Uncle Remus.** Illustrated by Jerry Pinkney. Dial Books, 1994. ISBN 0-8037-1303-7.

Julius Lester's warm, witty style and Jerry Pinkney's remarkable illustrations bring to life wonderful tales of Uncle Remus in this fourth volume of stories. In tales told with a modern southern dialect, Brer Rabbit, Brer Tiger, Brer Fox, Brer Lion, and Brer Bear, just to name a few, venture off in search of adventure. Learn why the Earth is mostly water. Hint: don't ever step on Brer Crawfish! *Multicultural.*

7.5   Napoli, Donna Jo. **The Magic Circle.** Dutton Children's Books, 1993. ISBN 0-525-45127-7.

Do you remember the evil witch in the classic children's story "Hansel and Gretel"? This imaginative story, told from the Ugly One's point of view, explores her rise and fall from revered village healer and dedicated mother to a lonely witch fighting her devilish impulses to eat the lost and vulnerable Hansel and Gretel. With a new twist on an old tale, this story examines the complex circumstances and emotions surrounding the witch's descent from good to evil.

7.6   Perrault, Charles (translated by Naomi Lewis). **Puss in Boots.** Illustrated by Stasys Eidrigevičius. North-South Books, 1994. ISBN 1-55858-099-9.

When the miller dies, his third son inherits only a small feline, Puss in Boots. But this cat is full of ideas. Just give him a bag and a pair of boots, and watch out! Though this is a well-known fairy tale, Stasys Eidrigevičius's illustrations help transform an old story into an exciting modern vision of magic.

7.7   Porte, Barbara Ann. **A Turkey Drive, and Other Tales.** Illustrated by Yossi Abolafia. Greenwillow Books, 1993. ISBN 0-688-11336-2.

Abigail and her brother, Sam, have inherited Dad's talent for storytelling and Mom's skill at painting and drawing. In this series of short, humorous vignettes, we become well acquainted with a family whose "quality time" is spent sharing oral histories and tall tales inspired by one another's artworks. A Chinese and a Mongolian tale offer an element of cultural diversity, although most of the tales are mainstream American in character. *Multicultural.*

7.8   Riordan, James. **Korean Folk-tales.** Oxford University Press, 1994. ISBN 0-19-274160-8.

Korea, the Land of the Morning Calm, is a magical, mystical place. Its most popular tales are about dragons, clever animals, or luckless people changed into unpleasant creatures. Discover how a long-nosed princess got that way, what is so special about a hare's liver, and how a loving daughter restored her father's sight. There are puzzling situations and wondrous adventures in these tales. *Multicultural.*

7.9 Ude, Wayne. **Maybe I Will Do Something: Seven Coyote Tales.** Illustrated by Abigail Rorer. Houghton Mifflin, 1993. ISBN 0-395-65233-2.

Coyote is a trickster, scapegoat, and hero in Native American mythology. In these seven tales he loses his eyes and finds new ones, tries to rob the sun, takes revenge on a rude village, and generally stirs up trouble for the people. The stories, all reinvented and reimagined by the author, explain Native American traditions. In the telling, the unique Coyote steals center stage every time. *Multicultural.*

7.10 Vuong, Lynette Dyer. **The Golden Carp, and Other Tales from Vietnam.** Illustrated by Manabu Saito. Lothrop, Lee and Shepard, 1993. ISBN 0-688-12514-X.

These delightful folktales from ancient Vietnam provide stories of humility, courage, friendship, and perseverance rewarded. The stories take place in pleasantly exotic settings where such characters as fierce dragons, brave heroes, and faithful friends face fearsome adventures, often with a surprise ending. Easy to read, the tales provide provocative comparisons with more familiar folktales and fairy tales. *Multicultural.*

7.11 Yolen, Jane, compiler. **Here There Be Unicorns.** Illustrated by David Wilgus. Harcourt Brace, 1994. ISBN 0-15-209902-6.

Through a collection of stories and poems, the mystery and romance of the unicorn come alive. Most beloved of all mythical beasts, the unicorn has always been a source of strength, purity, grace, and power. Elegant illustrations supplement writings from all over the world, past and present. *Multicultural.*

8 Friendship

8.1 Bennett, Cherie. **Sunset Fire.** Berkley/Splash Books, 1994. ISBN 0-425-14360-0.

When Emma's former boyfriend, Kurt, returns to Sunset Island, Emma is forced to make some decisions. She has lately been confiding in Pres, her best friend's boyfriend, and now her relationship with Samantha is in jeopardy. Emma is going to have to examine her priorities, reevaluate her friendships, and decide whether or not to get back together with Kurt in this book in the Sunset Island series.

8.2 Bridgers, Sue Ellen. **Keeping Christina.** HarperCollins, 1993. ISBN 0-06-021504-6.

Annie offers Christina friendship immediately when she enrolls in Annie's high school. Her longtime friends accept Christina but quickly become skeptical of the inconsistencies in her stories about her dead brother, her father's job, and her family's poverty. As the two girls spend more time together, Annie also begins to question Christina's truthfulness. Sue Ellen Bridgers realistically portrays the struggle for peer acceptance, along with loyalty and fidelity to family and friends.

8.3 Greene, Patricia Baird. **The Sabbath Garden.** Dutton/Lodestar Books, 1993. ISBN 0-525-67430-6.

For Opal Tyler, growing up as part of a dysfunctional family in a tenement on the Lower East Side of Manhattan is a daily struggle. The hardships of poverty, drugs, crime, and violence chip away at her self-esteem and confidence. Opie's hope is restored through her growing friendship with Solomon Leshko, an elderly Jewish man who lives downstairs. *Multicultural.*

8.4 Grover, Wayne. **Ali and the Golden Eagle.** Greenwillow Books, 1993. ISBN 0-688-11385-0.

Wayne Grover, an American engineer working in Saudi Arabia, comes to the remote village of Ezratu and befriends Ali, a shepherd. Villagers here live as their ancestors have for centuries. Using his mountain-climbing skills and equipment, Wayne captures and presents an eagle chick to Ali's father. Ali trains the magnificent eagle, Samson, to become a prized hunter. When Ali and Samson win a royal falconry contest, the isolated village of Ezratu is launched into the modern world. *Multicultural.*

8.5 Kehret, Peg. **The Richest Kids in Town.** Dutton/Cobblehill Books, 1994. ISBN 0-525-65166-7.

Having just moved to a new town, Peter Dodge is faced with finding a new friend. Of all the students in his fourth-grade class, Peter thinks Wishbone Wyoming III would make a good friend. Since both have a common interest—a need for money—they become involved in some money-making ventures that do not necessarily meet their common goals. However, their experiences do help cement their friendship.

8.6 Kincaid, Beth. **Back in the Saddle.** Berkley/Jove Books, 1994. ISBN 0-515-11480-4.

The first day at Silver Creek Riding Camp has been a disaster. Cabinmates Katie, Melissa, Jenna, and Sharon have already earned the name "Thoroughbrats" because of their persistent bickering. Before long, however, their better natures emerge, and they help each other to overcome the challenges of physical disability, racial tension, and impossible dreams. A book in the Silver Creek Riders series.

8.7 Lee, Marie G. **Saying Goodbye.** Houghton Mifflin, 1994. ISBN 0-395-67066-7.

Everything begins to fall in place for Asian American student Ellen Sung during her freshman year at Harvard. She has a great roommate, Leecia, and a sensitive boyfriend, Jae Chun Kim; and she manages to find time for her premed studies, creative writing, and tae kwon do class. While Ellen wrestles with the excitement of being away from home, she learns that life is filled with complicated decisions. She faces a time of unexpected confrontation and reconciliation with both people and ideas. *Multicultural.*

8.8 Paulsen, Gary. **Harris and Me: A Summer Remembered.** Harcourt Brace, 1993. ISBN 0-15-292877-4.

An eleven-year-old city boy with an unhappy home life is sent to spend the summer on his aunt and uncle's farm. Initially, he has misgivings, but his cousin, Harris, changes all that. Soon the routine of real farm life kicks in, and the boy does not notice the early hours, backbreaking chores, and huge, frequent meals. He is too busy moving from one escapade to another, with Harris leading the way. Whether it is launching an attack on 300-pound pigs or trying to beat off Ernie, the kami-kaze rooster, the events in *Harris and Me* provide a laugh a minute: hilarious, sad, wild, engaging.

8.9   Rochman, Hazel, and Darlene Z. McCampbell, compilers. **Who Do You Think You Are? Stories of Friends and Enemies.** Little, Brown/ Joy Street Books, 1993. ISBN 0-316-75355-6.

This collection of short stories by Sandra Cisneros, Tobias Wolff, Toni Cade Bambara, Louise Erdrich, Tim O'Brien, Gish Jen, and others explores the complex relationship we call *friendship* in new and often unsettling ways. Are there limits to a friendship? What happens when friendship blooms? What happens when it dies? Do friends and en-emies sometimes change places? These powerful stories offer many different answers.

8.10   Wallace, Bill. **True Friends.** Holiday House, 1994. ISBN 0-8234-1141-9.

Courtney feels great about herself. She has the right junior high friends, nifty clothes, the chance to work on cars with her father, and a brother she adores. Then her brother is jailed for possession of drugs, and her stepmother cleans out their bank account and leaves. When Courtney is accused of stealing "picture money" from her class, a physically disabled and ignored classmate befriends Courtney and teaches her how to recover her energy and sense of worth.

8.11   Werlin, Nancy. **Are You Alone on Purpose?** Houghton Mifflin, 1994. ISBN 0-395-67350-X.

Alison is a loner with an autistic twin brother who commands all of her parents' attention and requires constant defending. Harry, the rabbi's son, takes pleasure in tyrannizing Alison and her brother. When Harry is left paralyzed by a sudden accident, he and Alison are drawn to-gether. Both young people have deep anger about their own particular situation; they know how it feels to be on the outside looking in. How can they make peace with each other and their situations?

8.12   Williams, Vera B. **Scooter.** Greenwillow Books, 1993. ISBN 0-688-09376-0.

When Elana Rose Rosen moves to the Melon Hill apartments with her mother, her shaken sense of security threatens to keep her hiding in-side. However, a shiny new scooter soon lures her into the street and consequently into a fascinating new circle of friends and neighbors. Before long, Elana is an indispensable and well-loved member of a community struggling together against the hardships of single parenting, illness, aging, and growing up.

Boston Globe–Horn Book Fiction Award, 1994

8.13 Wittlinger, Ellen. **Lombardo's Law.** Houghton Mifflin, 1993. ISBN 0-395-65969-8.

Fifteen-year-old Justine's life is changed when a new family moves in across the street. In thirteen-year-old Mike Lombardo, Justine discovers a fellow movie bug who shares her passion for foreign and avant-garde films. Moreover, despite the gap in their ages, she realizes that Mike is more exciting to be with than any of her high school friends. As the two venture into a filmmaking project, Justine is forced to reflect on her true feelings for Mike.

9 Growing Up

9.1   Barrett, Elizabeth. **Freefall.** HarperCollins, 1994. ISBN 0-06-024465-8.

Seventeen-year-old Ginnie has plans for her summer, but they do not include spending the whole summer out of town with her grandmother. She learns that her parents are separating, and feels that she has been conveniently removed from home for the process. This painful and confusing summer has surprises in store for Ginnie, including romance.

9.2   Block, Francesca Lia. **The Hanged Man.** HarperCollins Children's Books, 1994. ISBN 0-06-024536-0.

Seventeen-year-old Laurel lives in the fast lane. Attempting to escape her dark past, she immerses herself in the heady rhythms of L.A. But the journey threatens to send her spinning out of control and crashing like the shattered glass that haunts her home. This is a moving story about survival and the triumph of friendship over despair. Reference to casual use of drugs and sexual experiences may be objectionable to some readers.

9.3   Block, Francesca Lia. **Missing Angel Juan.** HarperCollins Children's Books, 1993. ISBN 0-06-023004-5.

A tangly haired, purple-eyed girl named Witch Baby lives in Los Angeles, plays drums in a band, and loves a boy named Angel Juan. When Angel Juan goes to New York to find his own song, Witch Baby follows. She finds a guide in the big city, her ghostly almost-grandfather, Charlie Bat, who accompanies her through frightening, surreal adventures. Encountering fear and darkness, Witch Baby ultimately grows to recognize the power of love in this sequel to *Weetzie Bat.* Mature subject and language.

9.4   Calvert, Patricia. **Picking Up the Pieces.** Charles Scribner's Sons, 1993. ISBN 0-684-19558-5.

A motorcycle accident has left Megan confined to a wheelchair with what her therapists call SCI, spinal cord injury. One ride with a handsome senior, and her life has been changed forever. Determined to help her recover, Megan's family rents the lake cottage where they have always vacationed. There Megan becomes deeply involved with a boy she wants to dislike, learning about emotional as well as physical injury.

9.5 Choi, Sook Nyul. **Gathering of Pearls.** Houghton Mifflin, 1994. ISBN 0-395-67437-9.

Sookan Bak comes from Seoul, Korea, to attend a college in New York, despite her family's displeasure and her scant knowledge of English. She is respected by her professors for carrying a heavy class load and by new friends who admire her ability to work two jobs to pay her way. Sookan is torn between meeting her own expectations and those of her family. Must she return home at the end of college and join her sister as a nun? A sequel to *Year of Impossible Goodbyes* and *Echoes of the White Giraffe. Multicultural.*

9.6 Disher, Garry. **The Bamboo Flute.** Ticknor and Fields, 1993. ISBN 0-395-66595-7.

Paul dreams of a time when there was music in his life, before his family, like everyone else in Australia, became poor. His father no longer whistles, and the piano has been sold. All that is left is never-ending work and school. So Paul dreams. He meets a swagman, or drifter, who teaches him how to make a flute. Paul's music becomes the instrument through which he can communicate with others and with himself.

9.7 Gallo, Donald R., editor. **Within Reach: Ten Stories.** HarperCollins Children's Books, 1993. ISBN 0-06-021440-6.

This collection of short stories by current authors of young adult fiction is packed full of contemporary situations in which characters must make hard choices. They face real problems, like traveling alone to visit a parent in another state, learning to understand their cultural heritage, dealing with the temptation to cheat in school. The authors' styles and themes will appeal to young teenagers, especially those in grade nine.

9.8 George, Jean Craighead. **Julie.** Illustrated by Wendell Minor. HarperCollins Children's Books, 1994. ISBN 0-06-023528-4.

This sequel picks up the tale of *Julie of the Wolves.* After surviving on the Alaskan tundra for months, Julie returns to the modern world to face new challenges different from those she faced in the wild. Her father has married a non-Inuit woman, has forsaken many of the Inuit ways, and has even threatened to shoot Julie's wolves. Her village is no longer isolated from the outside world and has changed as well. A handsome stranger from Siberia complicates Julie's new life as she struggles to fit into her father's new family and to learn to live as a young adult in the modern world. *Multicultural.*

9.9   Geras, Adèle. **Pictures of the Night.** Harcourt Brace, 1993. ISBN 0-15-261588-1.

Pictures of the Night follows *The Tower Room* and *Watching the Roses* in a fairy-tale-inspired trilogy about three friends. In a contemporary version of "Snow White," eighteen-year-old Bella is enjoying a carefree summer in France before she begins college. Suddenly she finds herself threatened by two mysterious women who bear an eerie resemblance to her jealous stepmother.

9.10 LeMieux, A. C. **The TV Guidance Counselor.** William Morrow/Tambourine Books, 1993. ISBN 0-688-12402-X.

Michael must cope with his parent's divorce, his best friend's cruel practical jokes, his new job at Thumm's market, and his girlfriend, Melissa. He finds shelter and distance from these pressures behind the lens of his camera, a parting gift from his father. The more clearly Michael sees the world through a camera lens, the more detached from reality he becomes.

9.11 McColley, Kevin. **Pecking Order.** HarperCollins, 1994. ISBN 0-06-023554-3.

The Morrells have farmed this land in Minnesota for many generations, but now Dad cannot meet the financial demands. Young Tom sees his father struggle and wants to help, but he is distracted by falling in love for the first time. As Tom comes to grips with dramatic changes in his life, he discovers reserves of humor and energy he never knew he had. Mature language may be offensive to some readers.

9.12 Namioka, Lensey. **April and the Dragon Lady.** Harcourt Brace/ Browndeer Press, 1994. ISBN 0-15-200886-1.

In addition to balancing the demands of a busy senior year, April Chen tries to find a way to reconcile her loyalties to both Chinese and American values. In keeping with Chinese tradition, she is responsible for the care of her aging and cantankerous grandmother. On the other hand, her American upbringing has infected her with dreams of college, a career, and independence. April's father and friends help her find a solution to this dilemma. *Multicultural.*

9.13 Rubin, Susan Goldman. **Emily Good as Gold.** Harcourt Brace/ Browndeer Press, 1993. ISBN 0-15-276633-2.

Emily Gold knows she is different: she attends a special camp and a special school with other kids like her who are developmentally disabled. Like other thirteen-year-olds, she wants to wear heels and have her ears pierced, despite the fact that her father objects. As Emily struggles with adolescent situations and decisions, she and her father both come to a deeper understanding of what it means to truly care and to trust.

9.14   Rumbaut, Hendle. **Dove Dream.** Houghton Mifflin, 1994. ISBN 0-395-68393-9.

To thirteen-year-old Dove, Aunt Anna leads a wonderful life waitressing at Don's Truck Stop and dating the handsome Troy. Then Dove is sent to live with Aunt Anna while her parents get their lives back together, and a new world opens up for her. Learning to drive a car, waiting on tables, and falling in love, as well as learning about her Chickasaw heritage, make this a summer she will never forget. *Multicultural.*

9.15   Say, Allen. **The Ink-Keeper's Apprentice.** Houghton Mifflin, 1994. ISBN 0-395-70562-2.

Kivoi Sei's dream of becoming an artist draws him into the fascinating world of renowned Japanese cartoonist Noro Shinpei and his colorful apprentice, Tokida. Soon the sheltered young man's initiation into the artist's life reveals to him the harsher scenes of post-World War II Tokyo. Sei must survive a meal of fugu (a potentially lethal Japanese delicacy), a violent political demonstration, his first crush, and his matriarchal grandmother on his way to becoming Allen Say, the real-life author and illustrator. *Multicultural.*

9.16   Soto, Gary. **Jesse.** Harcourt Brace, 1994. ISBN 0-15-240239-X.

Seventeen-year-old Jesse leaves home in an attempt to escape from his alcoholic stepfather and an empty life; he goes to live with his older brother, Abel. Within the context of the Vietnam War, Richard Nixon's presidency, and Cesar Chavez's active struggle for farm workers' rights, Jesse and Abel attend a Fresno community college during the week and labor in the fields on the weekends. Together the Mexican American brothers struggle for economic independence and a positive identity. *Multicultural.*

9.17   Soto, Gary. **Local News.** Harcourt Brace, 1993. ISBN 0-15-248117-6.

This collection of short stories shows the lives of Mexican American young people in California today. Weasel bribes his younger brother, Angel, to do his chores by snapping a photograph of Angel in the shower. Eddie, the handsomest seventh grader in school, gives Lorena his Raiders jacket for the day, and she accidentally leaves it in biology class. Jose claims to be a racquetball champ to impress Estela, only to be embarrassed when she beats him 21–0 in a game. *Multicultural.*

9.18   Tamar, Erika. **The Things I Did Last Summer.** Harcourt Brace, 1994. ISBN 0-15-200020-8.

Andy has hopes for this summer before his senior year—journalism and sex. While spending these weeks with his stepmother on the island, he has an opportunity to work on *The Bay Island News,* and he meets Susan, a beautiful twenty-year-old. There is a mystery surrounding her; Andy is determined to find out what it is and to save her, if he can. Andy's hopes are not disappointed. He learns about himself, his family, and courage.

9.19   Thesman, Jean. **Cattail Moon.** Houghton Mifflin, 1994. ISBN 0-395-67409-3.

The mystery begins when Julia Foster moves from Seattle, and a mother who drives her crazy, to live with her father and grandmother in the small town of Moon Valley. Soon Julia is haunted by the ghostly figure and captivating songs of Christine Woodmark, a resident who died nearly twenty years ago. In this journey of romance and self-discovery, Julia learns just how important it is to follow your own dreams.

9.20   Williams, Michael. **The Genuine Half-Moon Kid.** Dutton/Lodestar Books, 1994. ISBN 0-525-67470-5.

Jay has a unique solution to his problems: stay underwater whenever possible. Submerged in the huge fish tanks at the hatchery seems to be the only place that's peaceful in his not-so-peaceful existence. His father is missing; his mother dates too much; and his grandmother has a decided taste for silver—she eats the silverware. A quest for possible treasure, left to him by his grandfather, brings Jay out onto dry land and into the world of people.

9.21   Yep, Laurence, editor. **American Dragons: Twenty-Five Asian American Voices.** HarperCollins, 1993. ISBN 0-06-021494-5.

In this collection of short stories, poems, and other selections, a winning combination of Asian authors offers glimpses of life for a young adult making the transition from Asian identity to the American Dream. In the face of hardships—from detention camps to stereotypes in high school—these teenagers from China, Japan, Korea, Tibet, Vietnam, and Thailand struggle with the same questions we all ask: Who am I? Where do I fit in? *Multicultural.*

10 Historical Fiction

10.1 Cushman, Karen. **Catherine, Called Birdy**. HarperCollins/Harper Trophy Books, 1994. ISBN 0-06-440584-2.

Catherine, a strong-willed fourteen-year-old, lives in England in the year 1290. In her diary she records the life of a knight's daughter in the Middle Ages: the boredom of endless sewing, joy of celebrations, fear of sickness, misery of learning how to be a "lady," and opposition to her father's determined attempts to marry her off to any elderly rich suitor. Catherine's adventures and her hopes and fears provide a revealing portrait of medieval times. See Richard Platt's *Stephen Biesty's Cross-Sections: Castle* (11.29) for a look at what kind of place was home in medieval times.

Newbery Honor Book, 1995

10.2 Dorris, Michael. **Guests.** Hyperion Books for Children, 1994. ISBN 0-7868-0047-X.

Angry at his father for inviting strangers to be guests at the harvest meal, Moss runs away into the forest. A raccoon and a young girl help him understand who he is now and what kind of man he may become. Michael Dorris shows us how the pilgrims may have been perceived by Indian families who invited them to share in the first Thanksgiving. As in his book *Morning Girl,* Dorris shows us a moment in history viewed from a new perspective.

10.3 Fleischman, Paul. **Bull Run.** HarperCollins/Laura Geringer Books, 1993. ISBN 0-06-021446-5.

In the tradition of Edgar Lee Masters's *Spoon River Anthology,* which contains elements of fiction and nonfiction, Paul Fleischman paints a portrait of the first battle of the Civil War from the point of view of sixteen characters. We see the glory, pain, horror, and heartbreak of war through the eyes of a doctor, an artist, a black soldier, a boy, a slave, a mother—to name just a few. The result is a rich tapestry of personal impressions, insights, and reflections as sixteen people consider the meaning of war and peace. *Multicultural.*

10.4   Macaulay, David. **Ship.** Houghton Mifflin, 1993. ISBN 0-395-52439-3.

In a blending of fact and fiction, present and past, a group of underwater archaeologists in the Caribbean discovers the remains of a sixteenth-century caravel, a small sailing ship. They collect, measure, record, clean, and preserve artifacts removed from this sea grave. Also included is the actual shipbuilder's journal from early 1500, describing construction of the ship and the dreams that accompany the vessel on its maiden voyage.

10.5   Mazzio, Joann. **Leaving Eldorado.** Houghton Mifflin, 1993. ISBN 0-395-64381-3.

In letters to her deceased mother, fourteen-year-old Maude recounts her struggles living in a New Mexico mining town during the 1890s. Abandoned by her father, who has left in search of Yukon gold, Maude finds work as a hired girl in a boardinghouse and survives with the help of a few friends. In the process, she discovers the hardships and personal breakthroughs associated with being poor, female, independent, and artistic in an era when her girlfriends are all seeking husbands.

10.6   Meyer, Carolyn. **Rio Grande Stories.** Harcourt Brace/Gulliver Books, 1994. ISBN 0-15-295876-2.

In this novel, a seventh-grade class in Albuquerque, New Mexico, is developing "Rio Grande Stories": their interviews and impressions of the lives, families, and cultures in their community. The students—from Native American, Hispanic American, African American, Jewish, and Anglo backgrounds—compile a book filled with ghost stories, legends, recipes, and traditions. In the process of discovering their past, the students find out about themselves and each other as well. *Multicultural.*

10.7   Meyer, Carolyn. **White Lilacs.** Harcourt Brace, 1993. ISBN 0-15-200641-9.

With little warning, Rose Lee's entire African American community of Freedomtown is ordered to relocate to a barren, reeking site on the outskirts of Dillon, Texas, in the 1920s because the white folks suddenly decide they need a park. Some of Rose Lee's people respond by moving out of the state; some submit to the relocation; and some, like Rose Lee's brother, revolt. However, it is Rose Lee who discovers the most redeeming strategy for dealing with the heartache of parting. *Multicultural.*

10.8   Rinaldi, Ann. **The Fifth of March: A Story of the Boston Massacre.** Harcourt Brace/Gulliver Books, 1993. ISBN 0-15-227517-7.

Boston is not an easy place in which to live in 1768, as tensions between British and Americans increase. Fourteen-year-old Rachel Marsh, an indentured servant of young lawyer John Adams and his wife, Abigail, finds herself torn between love for the Adams family and friendship she feels for British Private Matthew Kilroy. When Boston citizens riot on 5 March 1770, Matthew leads the British attack against the Americans. Rachel must help her friend and find her own place in an emerging nation.

10.9   Rinaldi, Ann. **Finishing Becca: A Story about Peggy Shippen and Benedict Arnold.** Harcourt Brace/Gulliver Books, 1994. ISBN 0-15-200879-9.

In Philadelphia of 1778, Becca is personal maid to spoiled, rich Peggy Shippen. Becca experiences the hardships of the Revolutionary War and the harsh realities of Valley Forge through her brother serving with General George Washington. Becca watches firsthand as General Benedict Arnold makes the transition from officer to traitor. She wonders how she will get out of this situation alive.

10.10   Turner, Glennette Tilley. **Running for Our Lives.** Illustrated by Samuel Byrd. Holiday House, 1994. ISBN 0-8234-1121-4.

Escape is a word no slave dares say aloud, but when young Luther finds the cave, his family has a chance to escape their life of slavery. Thus begins the long trek north to freedom for the Lawson family. Early in the journey, eleven-year-old Luther and his younger sister, Carrie, are separated from their parents. The journey is not only long, but lonely, as the two youngsters search for both freedom and their parents. A companion to study of the Underground Railroad. *Multicultural.*

10.11   Wisler, G. Clifton. **Jericho's Journey.** Dutton/Lodestar Books, 1993. ISBN 0-525-67428-4.

Twelve-year-old Jericho Wetherby looks forward to adventure when his family decides to move to Texas to start a new life in 1852. Jericho soon learns that adventure has its price, as his family encounters hardship and illness along the trail. This youngster, though small for his age, finds that courage, perseverance, and teamwork are the true measures of maturity.

10.12   Yep, Laurence. **Dragon's Gate.** HarperCollins, 1993. ISBN 0-06-022971-3.

Otter, a Chinese youth, is sent to America in 1867 to work with his father and uncle on the building of the transcontinental railroad in the Sierra Nevada range of California. Withstanding oppressive labor conditions and conquering daily brushes with death, Otter discovers personal courage and learns from his uncle that one "can either change things, or go on being changed by events." Here is a vivid portrait of immigrant Chinese life during a strife-filled era of American history. *Multicultural.*

Newbery Honor Book, 1994

11 History

11.1   Black, Wallace B., and Jean F. Blashfield. **Iwo Jima and Okinawa.** Crestwood House, 1993. ISBN 0-89686-569-X.

During World War II, 80,000 marines fought fiercely against Japanese troops for five days and struggled for four more weeks to gain control of the island of Iwo Jima, one of the Volcano Islands south of Japan. The United States fought for three months to take the island of Okinawa, largest of the Ryukyu Islands southwest of Japan, in order to set up a base close enough to launch an attack on Japan. Thousands of Japanese and Americans died in these costly battles. This volume is part of the World War II Fiftieth Anniversary series.

11.2   Burrell, Roy. **Oxford: First Ancient History.** Illustrated by Peter Connolly. Oxford University Press, 1994. ISBN 0-19-521058-1.

This reference book, covering the period of the Stone Age through the time of the Romans, uses a remarkable combination of photographs, drawings, maps, and charts to introduce the subject of ancient history. For example, artifacts are discussed and illustrated next to photographs of current cultures using many of the same techniques. The Greek legend of the Minotaur, half bull and half man, is told in a comic-book format. Variety of information and presentation make this a fine addition to any reference library.

11.3   Carrick, Carol. **Whaling Days.** Illustrated by David Frampton. Houghton Mifflin/Clarion Books, 1993. ISBN 0-395-50948-3.

The golden age of American whaling comes to life in this detailed text, which traces the history of the whaling industry to the present day. Stunning woodcut illustrations convey the backbreaking, often dangerous labor of those who hunt whales. Attention is also given to the convictions of those people who seek to preserve the whales. A dictionary of whaling terms and a selected bibliography are included.

11.4   Collins, James L. **Settling the American West.** Franklin Watts, 1993. ISBN 0-531-20070-1.

Through paintings, photographs, maps, and lively text, this book chronicles the pioneer spirit that permeated the American West between 1865 and 1900. Chapters include such topics as the Oregon Trail, building the transcontinental railroad, experiences of Chinese immigrants, silver and gold strikes from the Canadian Rockies to the Southwest, epic cattle drives across the plains, and the hardships and triumphs of farmers. A comprehensive bibliography is included for further explorations into this historical period. The poetry in Ann Turner's *Grass Songs* (15.5) is a fine companion.

11.5   Connolly, Peter. **Pompeii.** Oxford University Press, 1994. ISBN 0-19-917158-0.

Imagine going about your daily business when, with a sudden roar and rumble, your world becomes a smoking ruin of fire and ash. For the people of the ancient Italian city of Pompeii, Mount Vesuvius ended their world on 24 August A.D. 79. Preserved for all time under many feet of ash and not discovered until 1748, the city offers a remarkable look at everyday Roman life nearly 2,000 years ago. Mosaics, finely detailed drawings, maps, and photographs of preserved artifacts supplement the research.

11.6   Davidson, Rosemary. **Take a Look: An Introduction to the Experience of Art.** Viking, 1993. ISBN 0-670-84478-0.

This book introduces young people to the world of art in an easy-to-read and easy-to-understand way. The volume covers a wide range of cultures, periods, artists, and styles, giving examples of each and including thought-provoking questions. A colorful art time line at the end of the book offers a sense of the history of art. The author explains unfamiliar terms and includes a glossary. A valuable supplemental text for any art class.

11.7   Day, Malcolm. **The Ancient World of the Bible.** Viking, 1994. ISBN 0-670-85607-X.

Have you wondered if the Garden of Eden ever existed and where it might have been, or how the Israelites actually crossed the Red Sea? Here is a combination of historical research and speculation that considers answers to these and other questions. Lifestyles and customs are discussed and illustrated in an attempt to make this time in history come alive.

11.8   Garfunkel, Trudy. **On Wings of Joy: The Story of Ballet from the Sixteenth Century to Today.** Little, Brown, 1994. ISBN 0-316-30412-3.

In this history of ballet, dance lover Trudy Garfunkel explores the development of the art since its origins in the courts of sixteenth-century Europe. Garfunkel's book is replete with sketches of ballet's greatest personalities and most entertaining anecdotes and facts. Black-and-white photographs, poetry about dance, and a glossary of dance terms contribute to the usefulness and artistry of the book.

11.9   Goldish, Meish. **Crisis in Haiti.** Millbrook Press, 1994. ISBN 1-56294-553-X.

Here is a succinct history of Haiti, a Caribbean island nation troubled by the struggle for power since the arrival of Columbus on its shores 500 years ago. In this book in the Headliners series, author Meish Goldish discusses the recent regimes of the Duvaliers, Raoul Cedras, and Jean-Bertrand Aristide, which all involved the United States intimately. Concluding with the October 1994 return to power of democratically elected Aristide, the book anticipates a more hopeful future for a country characterized by upheaval and poverty.

11.10   Greene, Jacqueline Dembar. **The Chippewa.** Franklin Watts, 1993. ISBN 0-531-20122-8.

Through maps, photographs, and text, this book describes the culture, religion, and politics of the Chippewa Indians, one of the largest Native American tribes living in the northern United States and Canada on land surrounding the Great Lakes. Included are aspects of tribal life, the vision quest, autumn harvest, raising children, and tension between traditional culture and the realities of modern life. *Multicultural.*

11.11   Hamilton, Virginia. **Many Thousand Gone: African Americans from Slavery to Freedom.** Illustrated by Leo and Diane Dillon. Alfred A. Knopf, 1993. ISBN 0-394-82873-9.

Virginia Hamilton traces the history of slavery in America from the earliest slave trading through the growth of the Underground Railroad to the Emancipation Proclamation. *Many Thousand Gone* tells this history through the voices and stories of those who lived it. This exceptional contribution to African American history is a tribute to those who helped pave the way to freedom. *Multicultural.*

11.12   Haskins, James. **The March on Washington.** HarperCollins, 1993. ISBN 0-06-021289-6.

Here is an inside view of the 1963 March on Washington, D.C., by approximately 250,000 people demanding racial equality. Included are details of behind-the-scenes activities, from arranging for portable toilets to setting up a meeting with President John Kennedy. We see nationwide injustices and learn about the great men and women who worked for needed civil rights reform, from Rosa Parks to Dr. Martin Luther King Jr. Black-and-white photos show the planners, the history, and the march, an important event in the African American struggle for equality. *Multicultural.*

Notable 1994 Children's Trade Books in the Field of Social Studies

11.13   Kalman, Bobbie. **Eighteenth Century Clothing.** Crabtree, 1993. ISBN 0-86505-512-2.

Why did eighteenth-century women wear decorative patches on their faces? What is a "plumper"? How often did an eighteenth-century man bathe, and what did he use to clean his teeth? You will find amazing and amusing answers to these questions in this examination of American fashion in the eighteenth century. Cloth making, footwear, and hairstyles are presented as historical curiosities. Readers will develop a lasting sense of how it felt to dress for success in the era of the flea-infested powdered wig!

11.14   Kalman, Bobbie. **Nineteenth Century Clothing.** Crabtree, 1993. ISBN 0-86505-513-0.

Bustles, breeches, chignons, and gaiters are a few examples of the clothing, hairstyles, hats, and shoes worn by nineteenth-century American men, women, and children. From work clothes to high fashion, footwear to underwear, the apparel and accessories of frontier, rural, and urban Americans are described, accompanied by full-color illustrations and photographs.

11.15   Kent, Deborah. **The Titanic.** Children's Press, 1993. ISBN 0-516-06672-2.

This book in the Cornerstones of Freedom series is a simplified account of the 1912 sinking of the famous British ocean liner *Titanic* in the North Atlantic, killing more than 1,500 of the 2,200 people aboard. The iceberg that ripped the bottom out of the double-hulled, "unsinkable" ship on its maiden voyage was not supposed to pose a problem. Readers are reminded that the natural world has power beyond that of human beings. Through photographs, paintings, drawings, and clear text, readers are given details of this "Night to Remember."

11.16   Kent, Zachary. **World War I: "The War to End Wars."** Enslow, 1994. ISBN 0-89490-523-6.

How did World War I begin? A German submarine torpedoes the British ocean liner *Lusitania,* killing 1,198 passengers, 197 of them Americans. President Woodrow Wilson chooses peace over a declaration of war. But other international violence, including the assassination of Archduke Franz Ferdinand of Austria, disrupts this peace and eventually draws the whole world into a war that topples thrones and destroys countries. Photographs and maps complement the text, combining to show the horror and despair of war. A book in the American War series.

11.17 Kort, Michael G. **China under Communism.** Millbrook Press, 1994. ISBN 1-56294-450-9.

The world's most populated country has changed drastically over the centuries. This book focuses on the last half of the twentieth century, following the civil war that erupted in China at the end of World War II. Leaders from Mao Zedong to Deng Xiaoping are presented in text and photographs. Understanding the last major holdout of communism today is important, and this volume provides background information, supported by a glossary and further reading list.

11.18 Lawrence, Jacob. **The Great Migration: An American Story.** Illustrated by Jacob Lawrence. HarperCollins Children's Books, 1993. ISBN 0-06-023037-1.

Between 1916 and 1919, hundreds of African Americans left the South to find a better life in industrial cities of the North. American artist Jacob Lawrence, whose parents were part of this exodus, chronicles the migration in a series of sixty sequenced paintings. Lawrence's powerful verbal narrative accompanies the artwork, and Walter Dean Myers's poem "an appreciation" evokes the spirit of hope and determination that motivated the great migration. *Multicultural.*

11.19 Levine, Ellen, editor. **Freedom's Children: Young Civil Rights Activists Tell Their Own Stories.** Avon/Flare Books, 1993. ISBN 0-380-72114-7.

In this anthology of oral histories, thirty children of the Civil Rights movement tell their stories. Now adults, they recount the horrors of segregation, bombings, beatings, and murders in the American South. They also celebrate the heroic Freedom Rides, bus boycotts, and voter registration drives that ultimately brought about change for African Americans. Interviews with and photographs of people intimately involved provide an honest and shocking perspective on what happened during this turbulent period of American history. *Multicultural.*

Jane Addams Award, 1994
ALA Best Books for Young Adults, 1994
Booklist Editors' Choices, 1993
IRA Children's Book Award, 1994

Notable 1994 Children's Trade Books in the Field of Social Studies
School Library Journal Best Books, 1992

11.20 Madgwick, Wendy. **Citymaze! A Collection of Amazing City Mazes.** Illustrated by Dan Courtney, Nick Gibbard, Dean Entwistle, and John Fox. Millbrook Press, 1994. ISBN 1-56294-561-0.

Here is a collection of maps from famous cities past and present, offered as a series of puzzles to solve. Tour the ancient Forbidden City of Beijing, China, or make your way from Victoria Station to St. James's Palace in London. You will have a bird's eye view of cities while you read about buildings of interest along the way.

11.21 Maestro, Betsy. **The Story of Money.** Illustrated by Giulio Maestro. Houghton Mifflin/Clarion Books, 1993. ISBN 0-395-56242-2.

The story of money is the history of trade. Thousands of years ago people exchanged items they could spare for other items they wanted. However, as people began to travel great distances to trade, a variety of valuable substances—barley, salt, beads, gold, silver—began to be used as tools to represent payment for trade items. *Money* had been invented.

11.22 Marrin, Albert. **Cowboys, Indians, and Gunfighters: The Story of the Cattle Kingdom.** Macmillan/Atheneum, 1993. ISBN 0-689-31774-3.

Columbus brought cattle to North America. Along with them came an entire culture, captured by the phrase "the frontier," that is still celebrated in film and folklore. True stories about the Comanche, Wild Bill Hickok, Nat Love (one of many African American cowboys), Sitting Bull, Annie Oakley, Teddy Roosevelt, and others furnish insight into the way of life associated with the American West. Full-color and black-and-white illustrations, maps, and photographs provide background information.

Notable 1994 Children's Trade Books in the Field of Social Studies
School Library Journal Best Books, 1993

11.23 Martin, Ana. **The World Heritage: Prehistoric Stone Monuments.** Children's Press, 1993. ISBN 0-516-08386-4.

In Western Europe stand huge stone monuments, or megaliths, often arranged in a circular pattern. These chunks of stone are so enormous that moving them, even today, would be almost impossible. How did they come to be there? England's Stonehenge, one of the most famous, is wreathed in legend linking it to King Arthur and older Celtic tales. What was the purpose of these monuments? Explore Stonehenge and nearby Avebury, the exotic temple of Ggantija, and the underground hypogeum, or burial chamber, of Hal Safliene and decide for yourself.

11.24 McNeese, Tim. **America's First Railroads.** Crestwood House, 1993. ISBN 0-89686-729-3.

American railroads came about through the dreams of many early innovators such as Oliver Evans and William Strickland. Tracks were laid across America, usually with immigrant labor, thus encouraging settlement of the West. There were problems and accidents, as well as major developments like headlights and cattle catchers. Standard-gauge tracks were developed, and sand was used to solve the "grasshopper" problem.

11.25 McNeese, Tim. **West by Steamboat.** Crestwood House, 1993. ISBN 0-89686-728-5.

Meet Nicholas Roosevelt and his creation—the first steamboat to head west to New Orleans from Pittsburgh. Its maiden voyage on the Ohio River was eventful and successful. These floating palaces test the strength, courage, and endurance of brave men and women who keep them afloat, despite the ever-present dangers of earthquakes, fires, floods, snags, explosions, and treacherous, changing rivers. You will even bump into Mark Twain in this book in the Americans on the Move series.

11.26 Mettger, Zak. **Till Victory Is Won: Black Soldiers in the Civil War.** Dutton/Lodestar Books, 1994. ISBN 0-525-67412-8.

African American participation in the American Civil War is covered in detail in the six chapters of this book. Free blacks as well as escaped slaves wanted to fight for the Union. Rejected at first, these courageous men were eventually organized into formal fighting units. Photographs, a glossary, and a bibliography support facts in the text. It is a sad commentary on our society that these valiant soldiers were not treated with much more respect after the war than before. *Multicultural.*

11.27 Murphy, Jim. **Across America on an Emigrant Train.** Houghton Mifflin/Clarion Books, 1993. ISBN 0-395-63390-7.

When Robert Louis Stevenson was young, he set off from Scotland in the 1870s to join the woman he loved in California. His traveling companions were emigrants hoping to settle in the vast new territories of the American West. This book interweaves Stevenson's words with the history of the transcontinental railroad, revealing both the power and romance associated with steam travel and the profound, sometimes tragic, impact it had on all those whose lives it touched.

ALA Notable Books for Children, 1994
Booklist Editors' Choices, 1993
NCTE Orbis Pictus Award, 1994
Notable 1994 Children's Trade Books in the Field of Social Studies
School Library Journal Best Books, 1993

11.28   Nirgiotis, Nicholas. **Erie Canal: Gateway to the West.** Franklin Watts/ First Books, 1993. ISBN 0-531-20146-5.

The 363-mile Erie Canal was constructed in the 1820s across the state of New York between Albany, on the Hudson River upstream from New York City, and Buffalo, on Lake Erie in western New York. The canal provided a route through the Appalachian Mountains, thus connecting the eastern seaboard with what was then the western frontier. This book relates the conception, construction, and maintenance of this important waterway. While it has been replaced by the New York State Barge Canal, the Erie Canal remains a symbol of the spirit and attitudes of the country. Many drawings and photographs give added information.

11.29   Platt, Richard. **Stephen Biesty's Cross-Sections: Castle.** Illustrated by Stephen Biesty. Alfred A. Knopf/Dorling Kindersley, 1994. ISBN 1-56458-467-4.

With descriptive text and remarkable illustrations, a typical castle in the Middle Ages comes alive before your eyes. From the dungeons to the kitchens, from the manorial court to the battlements, each page is crammed full of details and amazing facts about castle life in times of both war and peace. In its era, the castle functioned as a mini-universe, full of intrigue and suspense. This remarkable book adds needed details to our understanding of the medieval world. See Karen Cushman's novel *Catherine, Called Birdy* (10.1) for a story of a girl who lived in a medieval castle.

11.30   Platt, Richard. **Stephen Biesty's Cross-Sections: Man-of-War.** Illustrated by Stephen Biesty. Alfred A. Knopf/Dorling Kindersley, 1993. ISBN 1-56458-321-X.

Imagine 800 men crammed together between eight levels of swaying deck on a British Royal Navy man-of-war, or warship, around 1800. Ten cross-sections of *H. M. S. Victory* include colorful illustrations and fascinating anecdotes explaining details of the ship and of a sailor's life. How did people fight battles, eat, bathe, wash clothes, and sleep with so many bodies all in the same place? It wasn't easy!

11.31 Sita, Lisa. **The Rattle and the Drum.** Illustrated by James Watling. Millbrook Press, 1994. ISBN 1-56294-420-7.

Native American culture is full of ritual. There are rituals for everyday, for initiation and healing, for love and the changing of the seasons. These rituals span many Indian nations, such as the Creek, Hopi, and Apache. The process of ceremony is an integral part of all civilizations. Thorough research and lovely illustrations make this interesting aspect of Indian culture come alive. *Multicultural.*

11.32 Stein, R. Conrad. **The Montgomery Bus Boycott.** Children's Press, 1993. ISBN 0-516-06671-4.

Rosa Parks really did not have any idea that her actions on that cool December day in 1955 would have national consequences. She chose to have a seat in the white section of the bus and was not willing to give it up to a late boarding white man. Reverend Martin Luther King Jr. organized the boycott of buses in Montgomery, Alabama, in reaction to her arrest. Clear photographs and simple text in this book in the Cornerstones of Freedom series offer the reader details of this event that helped to launch the Civil Rights movement. *Multicultural.*

11.33 Taylor, Richard L. **The First Flight across the United States: The Story of Calbraith Perry Rodgers and His Airplane, the Vin Fiz.** Franklin Watts/First Books, 1993. ISBN 0-531-20159-7.

The year is 1911, and aviation is in its infancy. No pilot has completed an airplane flight across the United States—at least not until Calbraith Perry Rodgers arrives on the scene. Trained by the Wright brothers, Rodgers accepts publisher William Randolph Hearst's $50,000 challenge to fly from coast to coast. Through adventurous chapters and actual photographs, this book charts Rodgers's dangerous and exciting journey.

11.34 Taylor, Richard L. **The First Solo Flight around the World: The Story of Wiley Post and His Airplane, the Winnie Mae.** Franklin Watts/First Books, 1993. ISBN 0-531-20160-0.

Wiley Post was blind in one eye, had only an eighth-grade education, and was unlicensed, yet he was the first to complete a solo airplane flight around the world, traveling 15,474 miles in the record time of seven days. Post learned to fly an airplane as a parachutist with a flying show and later gave flying lessons. This book describes his background as well as noteworthy events in aviation history, including his solo flight.

11.35 Walker, Paul Robert. **Head for the Hills! The Amazing True Story of the Johnstown Flood.** Illustrated by Gonzalez Vicente. Random House/Bullseye Books, 1993. ISBN 0-679-84761-8.

Through a careful blending of narrative, historical facts, maps, illustrations, and photographs, this work recounts one of the worst natural disasters in American history in which over 2,000 people died. *Head for the Hills!* chronicles the days and hours leading up to the Johnstown Flood of May 1889 and its tragic aftermath for this town in the Appalachian Mountains of Pennsylvania. The book also provides lists of interesting facts related to the flood, a bibliography for further research, and an index.

11.36 Wormser, Richard. **Hoboes: Wandering in America, 1870–1940.** Walker, 1994. ISBN 0-8027-8280-9.

Not just a cursory treatment of the subject, this is startling, in-depth research into the roving, homeless life of the "hobo" from the mid-1800s through the 1930s and 1940s. The realities of this lifestyle are shocking and reveal it was hardly the idyllic existence often portrayed on the screen. The book includes remarkable photographs and interviews with people for whom wandering was a way of life. A companion to John Steinbeck's *Grapes of Wrath* and other books on the Great Depression era.

11.37 Zeinert, Karen. **Those Incredible Women of World War II.** Millbrook Press, 1994. ISBN 1-56294-434-7.

This book details the role of women who served their country in World War II in the armed services, as doctors and nurses, and on the home front in war industries. Less widely publicized is the role of black women in this effort. The book includes firsthand accounts, a time line of events, and a bibliography.

12 How-to Books

12.1 Deem, James M. **How to Read Your Mother's Mind.** Illustrated by True Kelley. Houghton Mifflin, 1994. ISBN 0-395-62426-6.

If you have ever wondered whether you have psychic abilities, this guide to extrasensory perception is sure to enlighten you. In addition to defining such terms as *parapsychology, clairvoyance,* and *telepathy,* this book reviews myths and facts about ESP, true stories of people who have had ESP experiences, and ways to develop your own ESP powers. Also intriguing are the self-tests and ESP experiments that will reveal whether you can truly read your mother's mind.

12.2 Fleischman, Paul. **Copier Creations: Using Copy Machines to Make Decals, Silhouettes, Flip Books, Films, and Much More!** Illustrated by David Cain. HarperCollins, 1993. ISBN 0-06-021052-4.

Have you ever considered making your own greeting cards, postcards, letterhead, stamps, jigsaw puzzles, badges, bumper stickers, flip books, or even films? This book shows you how a duplicating machine can assist you in all of these projects and many more. Some of the ideas presented would make great gifts for friends and family. Instructions and illustrations are easy to follow. A chapter on necessary supplies is especially helpful.

12.3 Friedhoffer, Bob. **The Magic Show: A Guide for Young Magicians.** Illustrated by Linda Eisenberg. Millbrook Press, 1994. ISBN 1-56294-355-3.

This book starts off with some fine tips on how to put on a magic show, including an actual program of tricks, and then teaches you eighteen great tricks. There are even suggestions for music that you can use to enhance your performance and directions for building a portable magician's table.

12.4 James, Elizabeth, and Carol Barkin. **Sincerely Yours: How to Write Great Letters.** Houghton Mifflin/Clarion Books, 1993. ISBN 0-395-58832-4.

Here is everything you need to know about the lost art of letter writing for different purposes and in different formats. Engaging examples of thank-you notes, apologies, letters of condolence, invitations and replies, complaints, and other letters provide excellent models for the novice letter writer and also serve as useful refreshers for the more practiced correspondent. Discover just how versatile this means of communication can be. Whether you are sending for free items, cheering up a sick friend, writing to a pen pal in another country, or expressing an opinion, letters are an effective way to communicate.

12.5   Krizmanic, Judy. **A Teen's Guide to Going Vegetarian.** Illustrated by Matthew Wawiorka. Viking, 1994. ISBN 0-670-85114-0.

This friendly and informative guide, written especially for teenagers who want to "just say no" to meat, candidly details everything from individual reasons for becoming a vegetarian to how to handle parents and friends, social situations, and nutritional basics. The real facts regarding the cost of processing meat for human consumption, no-nonsense nutritional guidelines, sample menus, appealing recipes, and straightforward advice from vegetarian teens make this an invaluable resource for both confirmed and new vegetarians.

12.6   Levine, Michael. **The Kid's Address Book.** Berkley/Perigee Books, 1994. ISBN 0-399-51875-4.

Here are over 2,000 addresses of celebrities, athletes, entertainers, and more. In the opening "Author's Note to Kids," Michael Levine emphasizes that we all are accustomed to thinking in terms of one person, one vote. In reality, we vote our preferences and beliefs every day in the decisions we make, the products we buy, the music we listen to. This collection of addresses encourages us to get involved in the world and share our opinions by writing to others.

12.7   Ryan, Steve. **Test Your Math IQ.** Sterling, 1994. ISBN 0-8069-0724-X.

This collection of 78 math puzzles captures the mind's eye, engages the imagination, and expands powers of thought. Magic squares, devious dissections, tessellations, problems in topology, and other puzzles ask the reader to move beyond the basics of addition, subtraction, multiplication, and division. The puzzles vary in their degree of complexity and are rated with one, two, or three pencils to show complexity. An answer key can be found at the back of the book.

12.8   Stevens, Carla. **A Book of Your Own: Keeping a Diary or Journal.**
Houghton Mifflin/Clarion Books, 1993. ISBN 0-395-67887-0.

For anyone who has ever thought of keeping a diary or journal, this is
a wonderful place to begin. "What shall I write; who will read it; why
do I want to write?" These questions are answered in this book. Included are wonderful excerpts from the diaries of famous people, examples of codes invented to keep thoughts private, and reflections on
journal writing in general. There is also a discussion of some literary
techniques and examples from all over the world.

13 Issues of Our Time

13.1   Bauer, Marion Dane, editor. **Am I Blue? Coming Out from the Silence.** HarperCollins, 1994. ISBN 0-06-024253-1.

These sixteen original short stories explore aspects of growing up gay or lesbian or with gay or lesbian friends or parents. Written by respected young adult authors like M. E. Kerr, Bruce Coville, Lois Lowry, William Sleator, and Jane Yolen, the stories also help to dispel myths and stereotypes about homosexuality as they tackle the topics of love, coming of age, and self-identity.

13.2   Crutcher, Chris. **Staying Fat for Sarah Byrnes.** Greenwillow Books, 1993. ISBN 0-688-11552-7.

Eric Calhoune knows how his best friend, Sarah Byrnes, feels. All his life he has been taunted for being fat, while Sarah definitely lives up to her surname, "Burns." When Sarah was three years old, she was badly burned. The circumstances surrounding this incident remain a mystery, but everyone knows that her sinister father has never allowed her to have plastic surgery to repair the damage. Eric becomes involved in solving this mystery of Sarah's past in order to save his friend, which very nearly costs him his own life.

13.3   Disher, Garry. **Ratface.** Ticknor and Fields, 1994. ISBN 0-395-69451-5.

When Max and Christina discover that their adoptive parents belong to a white racist cult and that everything they have been taught about the world is a lie, they decide to run away. Ratface, their nickname for the cult's ranking official, is equally determined that they should stay. When the children break for freedom, they discover unexpected cruelty in Ratface and previously untapped resources within themselves.

13.4   Donovan, Stacey. **Dive.** Dutton Children's Books, 1994. ISBN 0-525-45154-4.

V's life begins to fall apart the morning a speeding hit-and-run driver injures her dog, Lucky. V's father is diagnosed with a terminal illness; her mother drinks more than ever; her best friend is strangely distant;

and V realizes she is entranced with Jane, a new girl at school. V must confront serious questions about life, death, relationships, love, and sexuality. Through loss and affirmation, V begins to realize the answers for herself. Mature treatment of lesbianism.

13.5   Garland, Sherry. **Shadow of the Dragon.** Harcourt Brace, 1993. ISBN 0-15-273532-1.

Sixteen-year-old Danny Vo lives in two worlds. In the world of his American high school, he is concerned with his science project and asking out Tiffany Schultz, who seems to like him. In the world of his Vietnamese family, Danny is responsible for helping his cousin, Sang Le, who has recently arrived from a Vietnamese re-education camp, get settled in school. When Danny's cousin joins a gang and meets up with Tiffany's skinhead brother, Danny's two worlds collide. *Multicultural.*

13.6   Hahn, Mary Downing. **The Wind Blows Backward.** Houghton Mifflin/Clarion Books, 1993. ISBN 0-395-62975-6.

Shy Lauren is surprised to find that beneath outgoing Spencer's seemingly happy exterior there is unhappiness and isolation, a dark side prone to moodiness and reckless behavior. Lauren and Spencer are drawn together and fall in love with an intensity that frightens them both. Lauren doubts if her love is enough to save Spencer from himself. The story deals with family conflicts, mental illness, and responsible sexual behavior.

13.7   Heneghan, James. **Torn Away.** Viking, 1994. ISBN 0-670-85180-9.

At age thirteen, Declan is smart, strong, self-sufficient—and a terrorist. His battleground is Belfast, Northern Ireland, and his enemy is the British. Deported to Canada for his endless fighting, Declan longs only to return to Ireland and avenge the death of his parents and sister. He must choose between a new life and vengeance. Choosing is not a simple matter.

13.8   Kerr, M. E. **Deliver Us from Evie.** HarperCollins Children's Books, 1994. ISBN 0-06-024475-5.

Sixteen-year-old Parr Burrman and his family face difficult times when word spreads through their rural Missouri town that his older sister is a lesbian. Evie has always been a loner, but she poses a dilemma for her traditional family when she leaves the family farm to live with the daughter of the town's banker. Parr, his older brother, and their parents must come to terms with Evie's lifestyle. It is then that Evie learns just how much her family loves her. The author deals sensitively and realistically with an important subject.

13.9   Kerr, M. E. **Linger.** HarperCollins, 1993. ISBN 0-06-022882-2.

Ned Dunlinger, owner of the town's best restaurant, Linger, requires the "proper" respect and obedience from his employees, his wife, and his daughter. Gary Peel and his family work at Linger, while his brother, Bobby, is fighting in the Persian Gulf. Lynn Dunlinger, Ned's beautiful daughter, falls in love and asks Gary to keep her secret. When Bobby returns home with his wounded buddy, Ned loses his iron control, hurting others and revealing himself as a patriotic bigot.

13.10   Lasky, Kathryn. **Memoirs of a Bookbat.** Harcourt Brace, 1994. ISBN 0-15-215727-1.

What happens to the children in a family when Mom and Dad become religious fanatics? To Harper, moving around has something romantic about it at first, though changing schools every few months is hard. Books are Harper's only real friends, but she must keep her reading a secret from her parents, who are opposed to reading because of their religious beliefs. Harper finds she is unwelcome in the family as her parents pursue increasingly narrower religious convictions, in which the end justifies the means.

13.11   Lowry, Lois. **The Giver.** Houghton Mifflin, 1993. ISBN 0-395-64566-2.

Jonas lives in an ideal world: there is no poverty, no conflict, no inequality. At the annual December Celebration, twelve-year-olds are given life assignments which match their interests, as determined by the elders. Jonas's assignment is to be Receiver of Memories from The Giver, to share in knowledge of the past in order to protect the community. Only The Giver and Jonas know what frightening truths shape this seemingly perfect community. An exciting and thought-provoking work that pairs well with *1984* or *Brave New World*.

ALA Best Books for Young Adults, 1994
ALA Notable Books for Children, 1994
Booklist Editors' Choices, 1993
Boston Globe–Horn Book Fiction Honor Book, 1993
IRA Children's Choices, 1994
IRA Teachers' Choices, 1994
Newbery Medal, 1994
Notable 1994 Children's Trade Books in the Field of Social Studies
School Library Journal Best Books, 1992

13.12 Lynch, Chris. **Gypsy Davey.** HarperCollins, 1994. ISBN 0-06-023586-1.

A product of child abuse and neglect, Davey becomes the self-appointed guardian of his own neglected nephew, Dennis. In spite of his sincere affection for the baby, Davey is unable to break the cycle of alcoholism, gang involvement, and single parenthood that plagues his family. Ultimately, a bicycle given to him by his absentee father allows him to roam far from his depressing home and becomes his sole consolation.

13.13 Lynch, Chris. **Iceman.** HarperCollins, 1994. ISBN 0-06-023340-0.

Eric's life is a mess! When he is not plastering his hockey opponents on the ice, he is lying in coffins and working part time for Mr. McLaughlin, an eccentric mortician. His father lives for Eric's victories on the ice, while his mother wants him to get serious about religion. Neither can give Eric the warmth and honest emotion he seeks, so he takes out his anger on the ice. Eric is heading for some real trouble unless he can find a constructive way to express his feelings. Subject matter may be objectionable to some readers.

13.14 Marsden, John. **Letters from the Inside.** Houghton Mifflin, 1994. ISBN 0-395-68985-6.

For two teenage girls, what could be more natural than to have a pen pal? At first, getting to know each other through letters and sharing secrets is fun. Then Mandy begins to notice that some details in Tracey's perfect life are not consistent; she discovers that Tracey is writing from a correctional institution. This revelation initially shocks Mandy, but it allows Tracey to be honest in what she writes. Now friends, the girls are determined to continue corresponding, sharing their fears and hopes and revealing the violence they face daily, Tracey in her life behind bars and Mandy with an abusive older brother. Suspenseful and terrifying, the story will stay with you.

13.15 Mazer, Anne. **The Oxboy.** Alfred A. Knopf/Borzoi Books, 1993. ISBN 0-679-84191-1.

In the olden days when people and animals lived side by side, the Oxboy would have fit in. Now he is an outcast and must keep his ancestry a secret. "No one can tell that I am the son of an ox. Like my father, I am hardworking and have a stubborn nature." *The Oxboy* addresses many of the issues facing us today: suspicion of strangers, fear of differences, shame. This simple allegory will haunt readers long after they finish the 100-page story. A companion to *The Crucible* or study of the Joseph McCarthy era.

13.16   McClain, Ellen Jaffe. **No Big Deal.** Dutton/Lodestar Books, 1994. ISBN 0-525-67483-7.

Janice's favorite teacher, Mr. Padovano, is being persecuted because of rumors that he is gay. Janice does not understand what the big deal is with his sexual orientation, but she sure knows what it is like to be less than popular at school. Being overweight, she herself has put up with much ridicule over the years. One thing is certain: Janice is not going to stand by while students, and her own parents, have Mr. P. fired.

13.17   Nolan, Han. **If I Should Die Before I Wake.** Harcourt Brace, 1994. ISBN 0-15-238040-X.

Starved for a sense of belonging and brainwashed by Brad, her neo-Nazi boyfriend, Hilary lies in the hospital in a coma after a motorcycle accident. In a dream state, Hilary transcends fifty years of time and space as she becomes Chana, a Jewish teenager in Poland during the Holocaust. Through this firsthand journey, Hilary's hatred is replaced with understanding and compassion for the courage and humanity of those who suffered horrors in World War II ghettos and concentration camps.

13.18   Paulsen, Gary. **Sisters/Hermanas.** Harcourt Brace, 1993. ISBN 0-15-275324-9.

The lives of Rosa, an illegal Mexican immigrant making her way alone as a teenage prostitute, and Traci, a wealthy American girl pressured by her mother to make all the right connections, briefly intersect in this bilingual novella with text in English and Spanish. Living alone in a rundown motel, Rosa works the streets in order to survive and help support her family in Mexico City, while Traci's life centers around popularity, fashion, and perfection. When the two girls accidentally meet, Traci suddenly understands just how similar their lives really are. Mature situation and language. *Multicultural.*

13.19   Qualey, Marsha. **Come In from the Cold.** Houghton Mifflin, 1994. ISBN 0-395-68986-4.

Jeff and Maud are two uncommon teenagers caught up in the political turmoil of the 1960s. Maud's radical sister has gone underground to protest the Vietnam War, and Jeff's brother, a marine, has just been called to combat duty. More than just a headline in the newspapers, the Vietnam War begins to shape their young lives. Surrounded by violence and despair, the two manage to find love and hope and decide to work for a better future.

13.20 Rapp, Adam. **Missing the Piano.** Viking, 1994. ISBN 0-670-85340-2.

Mike's parents are divorced, but Mike, his younger sister, Alice, and their mom have a happy, loving relationship. When Alice joins a traveling production of *Les Miserables,* Mom becomes her chaperone, so Mike must stay with his dad and a stepmother who dislikes him. Instead of playing on his high school basketball team, Mike is sent to a military academy, where he struggles to survive arbitrary discipline, bigotry, and brutality. Mature language and situations may offend some readers.

13.21 Rylant, Cynthia. **I Had Seen Castles.** Harcourt Brace, 1993. ISBN 0-15-238003-5.

Like many ordinary high school seniors in America in 1941, John Dante wants to enlist in the service so he can fight to win the war that began with the Japanese attack on Pearl Harbor. In the frenzy as the country prepares for war, John falls in love with Ginny, a girl opposed to war for any reason. In North Africa he experiences war and is changed forever. Though it is a deceptively short and simple story, mature language and vivid description give John's memories great emotional impact. A fine companion to *All Quiet on the Western Front, Slaughterhouse Five,* or *The Red Badge of Courage.*

13.22 Wolff, Virginia Euwer. **Make Lemonade.** Scholastic, 1993. ISBN 0-590-48141-X.

Fourteen-year-old Verna lives in the inner city and needs a job; she is going to be the first person in her family to go to college. Answering an ad for "Babysitter Needed Bad," she meets Jolly, a seventeen-year-old single mother of two toddlers who are "constantly leaking liquids everywhere." Verna struggles with her desire to help this family survive and with the dark side of growing up in poverty. Honesty of insight and a spare but elegant style bring alive this story of triumph of the human spirit. A companion novel to Langston Hughes's poetry.

ALA Best Books for Young Adults, 1994
ALA Notable Books for Children, 1994
ALA Quick Picks for Young Adults, 1993
Booklist's Top of the List, 1993
School Library Journal Best Books, 1993

13.23   Wright, Richard. **Rite of Passage**. HarperCollins, 1994. ISBN 0-06-023419-9.

This posthumously published novella by Richard Wright is set in Harlem during the 1940s. When fifteen-year-old Johnny Gibbs discovers that his family is really a foster family, he runs away in rage and pain, joining up with a street gang called the Moochers. His life is irrevocably changed as he witnesses and participates in the violent actions of his new "family." The book also includes an essay on Wright's fiction by Princeton professor Arnold Rampersad, as well as a chronology of key events in Wright's life. *Multicultural.*

14 Mystery

14.1 Arkin, Anthony Dana. **Captain Hawaii.** HarperCollins, 1994. ISBN 0-06-021508-9.

When Aaron Pendleton arrives on the Hawaiian island of Kauai on a family vacation, little does he know what adventures await him. An afternoon raft ride around the Na Pali Coast leads to a mystery involving secret caves, a severed hand, a buried map, an evil land developer, and a motley crew of islanders led by the eccentric Captain Dan. What Aaron thought would be a relaxing Hawaiian vacation turns into a battle to stay alive!

14.2 Byars, Betsy. **The Dark Stairs.** Viking, 1994. ISBN 0-670-85487-5.

Just down the street from the home of young Herculeah Jones is an old, mysterious house that the neighborhood kids have dubbed "Dead Oaks." Although Herculeah's mother, a private investigator, has ordered her to stay away, Herculeah just cannot resist the temptation to explore the town's legendary mystery. Along with Meat, her best friend, Herculeah discovers the house's mystery, which lurks at the bottom of the dark stairs. A book in the Herculeah Jones Mystery series.

14.3 Carris, Joan. **Stolen Bones.** Little, Brown, 1993. ISBN 0-316-13018-4.

Eleven-year-old Alec has two mysteries to solve during his summer on a dinosaur dig in Montana: the puzzle of the dinosaur bones that have been disappearing from the site, and the meaning of the strange entries about himself that he finds in his grandfather's diary. As an archaeologist and a detective, Alec finds a solution to each mystery.

14.4 Gilson, Jamie. **Soccer Circus.** Illustrated by Dee deRosa. Lothrop, Lee and Shepard, 1993. ISBN 0-688-12021-0.

Everything seems to happen to young Hobie Hanson. He has promised his dad he will stay out of trouble. But when his soccer team goes out of town for the big tournament, Hobie finds himself in the middle of a fake murder mystery and a clown in a wedding. On top of this, the huge goalie from another team will not leave him alone. Trying to survive, Hobie learns some valuable lessons.

14.5   Heisel, Sharon E. **Wrapped in a Riddle.** Houghton Mifflin, 1993. ISBN 0-395-65026-7.

GrandAnn's inn, The Jumping Frog, becomes eleven-year-old Miranda's temporary home while her parents are away in Antarctica researching algae. Upset at switching schools and missing her parents, Miranda finds her lonely feelings are suddenly overpowered by strange happenings. A bust of Mark Twain falls on Mrs. Prescott, and then GrandAnn's precious letters written by Samuel Clemens turn up missing. As Miranda tries to solve the mystery, she meets new friends at school who agree to help.

14.6   Lasky, Kathryn. **A Voice in the Wind.** Harcourt Brace, 1993. ISBN 0-15-294103-7.

Liberty, July, Charly, and Molly Starbuck are two sets of twins with amazing telepathic abilities and a nanny who is both understanding and extraordinarily resourceful. Transplanted to New Mexico, where their father is involved in a controversial river diversion project, the twins discover both the charm of their surroundings and some strange happenings, including a murder. Their determination to solve these mysteries makes the story informative, suspenseful, and inspirational. A book in the Starbuck Family Adventure series.

14.7   Pfoutz, Sally. **Missing Person.** Viking, 1993. ISBN 0-670-84663-5.

Carrie's life is shaken to its foundations when her mother fails to return home one night. All Carrie has is a note from her mother saying, "I've gone to the movies." Now Carrie must deal with her father's and sister's reactions to her mother's disappearance and must sort out her own feelings for her mother. Carrie finds herself in a web of mystery with puzzling clues and strange characters.

14.8   Stine, Megan, and H. William Stine. **The Mummy Awakes.** Illustrated by Peter Peebles. Random House/Bullseye Chillers, 1993. ISBN 0-679-84193-8.

Cameron Ross cannot understand why the mummy of Neshi wants to kill him. Plagued by nightmares and stalked by the spirit of the young Egyptian, Cameron begins to fall apart. Even his mother, a famous Egyptologist, will not believe his claim that Neshi is alive until she sees for herself the empty coffin in the museum. Gradually, however, Cameron discovers what Neshi is really after, and he comes to terms with the fears that haunt him.

14.9 Wallace, Bill. **Blackwater Swamp.** Holiday House, 1994. ISBN 0-8234-1120-6.

When eleven-year-old Ted and his family move to Louisiana, Ted is faced with finding new friends. Jimmy seems to be okay, although Ted does not quite trust him. However, Jimmy is willing to go into the swamp with Ted to look for the mysterious witch. Ted is fascinated with the old woman and her love for the wild creatures of the swamp. When Jimmy starts the rumor that the witch is responsible for the town's recent break-ins, Ted is faced with a decision that could mean death to his baby sister.

15 Poetry

15.1 Feelings, Tom, editor. **Soul Looks Back in Wonder.** Illustrated by Tom Feelings. Dial Books, 1993. ISBN 0-8037-1001-1.

This beautiful celebration of African American heritage pairs poetry by Maya Angelou, Langston Hughes, Alice Walker, and other celebrated poets with captivating illustrations by Tom Feelings. Filled with a spirit of pride, strength, and endurance, this collection of thirteen poems connects young African Americans with their collective history and creative power, in the hope that "our previous young African sisters and brothers, who are our today and our tomorrow . . . see their own beauty reflected in our eyes, through our work." *Multicultural.*

ALA Best Books for Young Adults, 1994
ALA Quick Picks for Young Adults, 1994
Coretta Scott King Award for Illustration, 1994

15.2 Gordon, Ruth, editor. **Peeling the Onion: An Anthology of Poems.** HarperCollins/Charlotte Zolotow Books, 1993. ISBN 0-06-021727-8.

"Like the onion, poetry is a constant discovery." This collection of poetry selected especially for young people contains poems ranging in subject from "The Family Car" and "Body Surfing" to "Grandfather Talk" and "Braiding My Sister's Hair." Well-known poets such as Theodore Roethke, Octavio Paz, Gabriela Mistral, and Adrienne Rich refresh the reader with images of places, people, animals, and events in poems translated from Spanish, Yiddish, Korean, French, Russian, Papago, and Romanian. *Multicultural.*

15.3 Myers, Walter Dean. **Brown Angels: An Album of Pictures and Verse.** HarperCollins, 1993. ISBN 0-06-022917-9.

Walter Dean Myers has compiled turn-of-the-century photographs of African American children, which he found in antique shops, and has written biographical poems in a variety of styles to catch the spirit of each unknown child. He has created a touching album of photos and verse that displays his warm, personal view of his subject. *Multicultural.*

ALA Notable Books for Children, 1994

15.4 Rylant, Cynthia. **Something Permanent.** Photographs by Walker Evans. Harcourt Brace, 1994. ISBN 0-15-277090-9.

This remarkable combination of poetry by Cynthia Rylant and photographs by Walker Evans records the Great Depression era with startling empathy. Rylant's poems, each paired with a photograph, are so poignant that they bring tears to the eye—not so much tears of sorrow, although these were very difficult times, as tears of joy for something said just exactly right. The joining of art by these two people is art at its best, offering the reader a vivid portrait of a bygone era. A fine companion to study of the Great Depression.

15.5 Turner, Ann. **Grass Songs.** Illustrated by Barry Moser. Harcourt Brace Jovanovich, 1993. ISBN 0-15-636477-8.

In the voices of nineteenth-century pioneer women, these seventeen poems chronicle the beauty and pain of their experiences as they headed west. Stories of pregnancy and childbirth, encounters with Native Americans, the freedom of the wilderness, illness, death, the constant push to move onward—all unfold in these personalized perspectives. Inspired by the private journals of pioneer women, Ann Turner's poems present a tribute to the determination of these women to survive and forge a new life in an unknown place. An excellent companion to study of the westward movement in America.

15.6 Watson, Jerry, and Laura Apol Obbink, compilers. **Learning to Live in the World: Earth Poems by William Stafford.** Harcourt Brace, 1994. ISBN 0-15-200208-1.

"His love for the earth, for its inhabitants, and for life itself resonates on every page." To read these poems by William Stafford is to glow with a sense of belonging to the Earth and to one another. At times deceptively simple and reflecting both a gentle and fierce mood, the poems are grouped into sections representing different aspects of our relationship to the world. Readers can open the volume anywhere and smile in recognition of a friend reaching out.

16   Science

16.1   **Action Pack: Dinosaur.** Alfred A. Knopf/Dorling Kindersley, 1994. ISBN 1-56458-683-9.

Want to build a dinosaur? With this kit you can build a model of a stegosaur skeleton more than two feet long. Maybe you would rather follow a time line showing when dinosaurs lived, or play a game about dinosaurs. The Action Pack makes this possible. Both popular and far-fetched theories of why dinosaurs disappeared are included in this innovative kit.

16.2   **Action Pack: Night Sky.** Alfred A. Knopf/Dorling Kindersley, 1994. ISBN 1-56458-685-5.

This interactive kit leads you on a journey through the night sky. You learn about stars, planets, and black holes; you learn to recognize the constellations with the help of the Night Sky Guidebook. There are glow-in-the-dark stickers to paste on your ceiling and view with the lights out. While not an in-depth study of stars and planets, the *Night Sky* is an interesting and informative display.

16.3   **Action Pack: Pyramid.** Alfred A. Knopf/Dorling Kindersley, 1994. ISBN 1-56458-684-7.

Explore the tombs of ancient Egyptian kings with this interactive kit. Examine some of the treasures that were buried with the kings. Write a secret message using hieroglyphics or build an ancient pyramid. All of this and more is included in the Action Pack.

16.4   Asimov, Isaac, and Robert Giraud. **The Future in Space.** Gareth Stevens, 1993. ISBN 0-8368-0913-0.

How will future technology help us make new discoveries in space? The authors discuss proposed explorations of the twenty-first century, as well as the details of telescopes, shuttles, airplanes, and space stations. Clear and colorful illustrations abound as space issues such as extraterrestrial life forms, the Big Bang theory, and the speed of stars are explained.

16.5 Brandenburg, Jim (edited by JoAnn Bren Guernsey). **Sand and Fog: Adventures in Southern Africa.** Walker, 1994. ISBN 0-8027-8233-7.

This large-format book shows readers the unusual land of the Namib Desert in Namibia, formerly South-West Africa. Beautiful photographs and clear text focus on the animals, environment, and people of this harsh and unique strip of land on the southwest African coast.

16.6 Branley, Franklyn M. **Venus: Magellan Explores Our Twin Planet.** HarperCollins, 1994. ISBN 0-06-020298-X.

Imagine a world with no water, where the temperature day and night is hot enough to melt lead. This is what the planet Venus is like. Clouds of yellow have hidden its surface from our gaze for years. Now *Magellan,* the first planet probe to be carried aloft by a space shuttle, provides detailed pictures and information about our sister planet, Venus. Theories about the origin and evolution of Venus combine with new data to give us more knowledge about Earth.

16.7 Burnie, David. **Dictionary of Nature.** Alfred A. Knopf/Dorling Kindersley, 1994. ISBN 1-56458-473-9.

Beautifully illustrated, this reference guide contains informative material about life science. Included are biographies of many scientists who have contributed to the study of living things. All the basic areas of biology are covered, including genetics, evolution, classification, and ecology, to name a few.

16.8 Burnie, David. **Life.** Alfred A. Knopf/Dorling Kindersley, 1994. ISBN 1-56458-477-1.

What is life? This Eyewitness Science book poses the question and sets out to answer it, from the microscopic world of cells and how DNA works to interaction between the species. A combination of photographs, charts, illustrations, and diagrams takes readers to the past, the present, and the future, interrelating information and making connections with many aspects of life. Whatever your interest, from various theories of evolution to the use of the senses, this book is the place to begin.

16.9 Butterfield, Moira. **Space.** Illustrated by Nick Lipscombe and Gary Biggin. Alfred A. Knopf/Dorling Kindersley, 1994. ISBN 1-56458-682-0.

This book in the Look Inside Cross-Sections series invites readers into the interiors of space vehicles such as the *Apollo Lunar Module, Skylab,* and *Voyager* space probes. A short history of each vessel's service and descriptions of its technical features accompany each illustration. Included are a helpful glossary and a Space Timeline, which charts human involvement in space exploration in this century.

16.10   Cobb, Vicki. **Science Experiments You Can Eat.** Illustrated by David Cain. HarperCollins, 1994. ISBN 0-06-023534-9.

Why is one cookie crispier than another, and why don't they stay that way? Here is a chance to experiment and find out. This book is full of "tasty" experiments illustrating scientific principles. Each begins with a general premise, lists materials and equipment, and presents procedures and observations. These are simple and fun experiments that will encourage readers to think beyond the experiment itself to applications of the principles. A glossary at the end of the book explains scientific terms.

16.11   Cobb, Vicki, and Josh Cobb. **Light Action! Amazing Experiments with Optics.** HarperCollins, 1993. ISBN 0-06-021436-8.

A good supplemental text for a science classroom or an easy-reading technical book for outside reading, this book explains what light is and explores the basic principles of optics through experiments. Interesting experiments offer students a chance to extend their understanding of light.

16.12   **Eyewitness Encyclopedia of Science.** Alfred A. Knopf/Dorling Kindersley Multimedia, 1994. ISBN 1-56458-904-8.

This encyclopedia in CD-ROM format lets the viewer explore four main science subjects—math, physics, chemistry, and life science—in an interactive way. With the help of audio, video, and animation, the reader can access information about famous people, play a quiz master game for fun, or check through a who's who section. Words that may be unfamiliar are in red and can be clicked on for immediate definitions. This is a fun way to learn science concepts.

16.13   Ford, Michael Thomas. **One Hundred Questions and Answers about AIDS: What You Need to Know Now.** William Morrow/Beech Tree Books, 1993. ISBN 0-688-12697-9.

This is a well-organized, sensible, informative book containing a list of questions and answers about AIDS arranged like a table of contents. Here are all the details an ordinary person would want to know about AIDS. Included are interviews with AIDS victims and lists of organizations and hotlines dealing with the killer virus. This paperback is essential reading for young people.

16.14 Ganeri, Anita. **The Oceans Atlas.** Illustrated by Luciano Corbella. Alfred A. Knopf/Dorling Kindersley, 1994. ISBN 1-56458-475-5.

This large-format book covers virtually everything about the Earth's seas. Underwater landforms, island creation, reefs, marine biology, waves, and exploration are only some of the topics discussed in this easy-to-read volume. How was the Mariana Trench formed, or how do currents begin? Find out in this book. Colorful illustrations are the featured mode of presenting information in this volume for the home, library, or science classroom.

16.15 Gardner, Robert, and David Webster. **Science Projects about Weather.** Enslow, 1994. ISBN 0-89490-533-3.

Have you have ever wanted to make a cloud, a liquid tornado, or a weather-related project? This volume provides the necessary informa-tion. In addition to offering scientific explanations for phenomena such as temperature, snow, rain, wind, and storms, the book presents easy-to-follow and safe instructions for a variety of weather-related science projects. Diagrams, graphs, and photographs enliven the text.

16.16 Gowell, Elizabeth Tayntor. **Sea Jellies: Rainbows in the Sea.** Franklin Watts/New England Aquarium Books, 1993. ISBN 0-531-15259-6.

Did you know that sea jellies have lived on Earth for millions of years and that some can even be found in fresh water? Researchers are study-ing the chemicals in some jellies for possible treatment of cancer and other diseases. It is becoming clear that not only are these simple crea-tures beautiful and fun to watch, but they also play an important role in the chain of life in the oceans.

16.17 Gribbin, John, and Mary Gribbin. **Time and Space.** Alfred A. Knopf/ Dorling Kindersley, 1994. ISBN 1-56458-619-7.

Why do things wear out? What is a black hole? Many of the mysteri-ous questions we have about time and space are answered in this beau-tifully illustrated Eyewitness Science book. Full-color photographs of original scientific equipment, experiments, and 3-D models reveal dis-coveries made by past and present scientists in an informative, visual guide.

16.18 Halpern, Robert R. **Green Planet Rescue: Saving the Earth's En-dangered Plants.** Franklin Watts/Cincinnati Zoo Books, 1993. ISBN 0-531-11095-8.

What is an endangered species? Can plants be endangered species, too? You bet they can. Robert Halpern discusses just how important plants are to our world and what we can all do about saving the many species that are endangered right now. After all, directly or indirectly, all life on Earth depends on plants.

16.19   Johnstone, Michael. **Cars.** Illustrated by Alan Austin. Alfred A. Knopf/ Dorling Kindersley, 1994. ISBN 1-56458-681-2.

This collection of cross-sectional illustrations offers a new perspective on a popular subject: cars. Anecdotes about the evolution of the automobile and details about each vehicle's unique features accompany each colorful cross-section. The eleven illustrations in this book in the Look Inside Cross-Sections series are followed by a Car Timeline, which chronicles some of the major advances in automotive technology throughout the years.

16.20   Landolphi, Suzi. **Hot, Sexy and Safer.** Berkley/Perigee Books, 1994. ISBN 0-399-51882-7.

Sex educator Suzi Landolphi presents a frank but humorous examination of issues important to young adults who are or will become sexually active. Although promoting "safe sex" is Landolphi's primary concern, her work is equally valuable as a manual on self-esteem and personal empowerment. Since this book openly discusses sexual intercourse, masturbation, homosexuality, contraception, and sexually transmitted diseases, parental guidance is suggested.

16.21   Lippincott, Kristen. **Astronomy.** Alfred A. Knopf/Dorling Kindersley, 1994. ISBN 1-56458-680-4.

This Eyewitness Science book allows the reader to go from the general to the specific on each page. With skill and imagination, the Eyewitness team has opened the world of astronomy and science of the stars through writing, photography, drawings, and more. Theories we now take for granted are explored in their infancy, as are those theories that were taken for common truth many years ago but that have now been discarded. The excitement of the stars is found in this book.

16.22   Macaulay, David. **The Way Things Work.** Alfred A. Knopf/Dorling Kindersley Multimedia, 1994. ISBN 1-56458-901-3.

David Macaulay's popular book is now in CD-ROM format. See machines come to life through animation, audio, and wonderful illustrations. Simply by pointing and clicking, viewers explore machines, the scientific principles of how things work, the history of machines, and stories of the inventors. This is not an in-depth study, but it is certainly entertaining.

Boston Globe–Horn Book Nonfiction Award, 1989 (for the book)

16.23 McKeever, Susan, editor. **The Dorling Kindersley Science Encyclopedia.** Alfred A. Knopf/Dorling Kindersley, 1994. ISBN 1-56458-328-7.

This science encyclopedia is a one-volume treasure of scientific knowledge. Information is organized into major topics such as matter, reactions, ecology, and space. Within each topic is a wealth of facts, complemented by color photographs, diagrams, and charts. Biographical notes, time lines, a fact-finder section, and a glossary help put into context a massive amount of detail.

16.24 Parker, Steven. **Human Body.** Alfred A. Knopf/Dorling Kindersley, 1993. ISBN 1-56458-325-2.

If you have ever wondered what makes a human being "tick," this Eyewitness Science book will help you find out. Detailed pictures and drawings take you through the anatomy of the human body. More than that, there is also an explanation of how everything actually works. There are pictures and descriptions of the progression of medicine, with some fun anecdotes about historic beliefs and treatments.

16.25 Parker, Steven. **Natural World.** Alfred A. Knopf/Dorling Kindersley, 1994. ISBN 1-56458-719-3.

Here is another gem in the collection of Eyewitness Science books. This time the subject is the entire animal kingdom, including an extensive section on the history of life, from earliest reptiles to mammoths and mastadons. As always, illustrations and photographs are varied, detailed, and interesting, covering both past and present theories. Whether your interest is in how different animals hunt, their cycles of courtship, birth, and death, or their techniques for survival, this is the reference book for you.

16.26 Patent, Dorothy Hinshaw. **The Vanishing Feast: How Dwindling Genetic Diversity Threatens the World's Food Supply.** Harcourt Brace/Gulliver Green Books, 1994. ISBN 0-15-292867-7.

In the middle of winter in 1942, during the height of World War II, ten scientists starved to death surrounded by seed packets of varieties of corn, peas, rice, and many other edibles because they understood the need for "seed variety" to protect the world's food resources from extinction by diseases. These threats are even greater today. Can we prevent our own famine and extinction? Short, clear chapters present information about the importance of maintaining our biological diversity.

16.27 Platt, Richard. **Smithsonian Visual Timeline of Inventions.** Alfred A. Knopf/Dorling Kindersley, 1994. ISBN 1-56458-675-8.

The wonderful world of inventions is presented here in a time line complete with a variety of illustrations and inserts. There is general discussion of large inventions—such as steam engines and electric power—and the industrial revolution, as well as individual discussion of everything from microphones to a paper bag machine. The book is divided into categories of world events, travel and conquest, agriculture and industry, daily life and health, and courting and communications.

16.28 **The Ultimate Human Body: A Multimedia Guide to the Body and How It Works.** Alfred A. Knopf/Dorling Kindersley Multimedia, 1994. ISBN 1-56458-900-5.

Here is a multimedia guide to the human body and how it works in CD-ROM format. Watch a heart beat, listen to terms of the body with which you may not be familiar, learn why we do certain things like chew our food, or just browse around through the functions of the body and its organs. This CD is a colorful, illustrative way to investigate the functions of the human body.

16.29 Van Rose, Susanna. **Earth.** Alfred A. Knopf/Dorling Kindersley, 1994. ISBN 1-56458-476-3.

This volume in the Eyewitness Science series uses short, technical text supported by photographs, charts, and diagrams to introduce topics such as continental drift, plate tectonics, ocean floor formation, and erosion. This reference book explains what the Earth is made of, why it works the way it does, and how it continuously changes. Biographies of pivotal scientists are included, as are historical landmarks in the studies of geology, oceanography, paleography, and seismology.

16.30 **The Visual Dictionary of the Earth.** Alfred A. Knopf/Dorling Kindersley, 1993. ISBN 1-56458-335-X.

Everything you need to know about our world is contained in this book in the Eyewitness Visual Dictionaries series. Well, maybe not *everything,* but in these pages are volcanoes, trade winds, minerals and gems, oceans, earthquakes, and much more. Everything seems to be connected in this wonderful world of ours. Great photos and illustrations make Earth come alive for the reader.

16.31   Vogt, Gregory L. **The Search for the Killer Asteroid.** Millbrook Press, 1994. ISBN 1-56294-448-7.

Though it reads like science fiction, this book is pure fact. As you enter the world of asteroids, you discover how the "killer" is linked to the disappearance of dinosaurs sixty-five million years ago. Geologist "detectives" trace the formation of the Earth into the planet on which we live today. Realistic drawings and photographs help readers visualize this process. Whether you are interested in science or just curious about Earth's beginnings, this story is fascinating.

17 Society

17.1 Angelou, Maya. **Wouldn't Take Nothing for My Journey Now.** Random House, 1993. ISBN 0-679-42743-0.

In this collection of short essays, poet and writer Maya Angelou explores issues and concerns of being a woman in the 1990s. Spirituality, humor, individual style, risk taking, cultural and ancestral pride, relationships, sensuality, and pregnancy are among the topics Angelou addresses as she celebrates the triumphs and challenges of being a woman. This is an excellent companion to Angelou's autobiographical novels. Mature content.

17.2 Archer, Jules. **Rage in the Streets: Mob Violence in America.** Illustrated by Lydia J. Hess. Harcourt Brace/Browndeer Press, 1994. ISBN 0-15-277691-5.

What are the causes of riots, and how does a gathering become a mob? This book traces mob violence from the period immediately following the American Revolution up to the 1992 riots in Los Angeles. Author Jules Archer discusses general causes of mob violence, such as intolerance, racial prejudice, unemployment, and despair. Included is information about igniters of riots, such as court decisions, police oppression, taxation, and even problems at rock concerts. Each chapter is faced by an appropriate block print, and the volume offers a clear picture of how and why riots happen.

17.3 Atkin, S. Beth. **Voices from the Fields: Children of Migrant Farmworkers Tell Their Stories.** Little, Brown, 1993. ISBN 0-316-05633-2.

In their own words through interviews and in photographs, migrant workers' children tell of their lives, why they are here, how they live, and what they hope to accomplish during their lives. These young people are often separated from their families, their customs, and their remembrance of a native land. Their voices and faces are a haunting reminder of the alluring promise of America versus harsh reality. The text is printed in both English and Spanish. *Multicultural.*

17.4 Bachrach, Susan D. **Tell Them We Remember: The Story of the Holocaust.** Little, Brown, 1994. ISBN 0-316-07484-5.

Drawing on the United States Holocaust Memorial Museum's collection of artifacts, photographs, maps, and taped oral and video histories, this book tells the story of the Holocaust and how it affected the daily lives of innocent people thoughout Europe. Powerful stories and images are presented with the hope that these terrible crimes will never be forgotten or repeated.

Booklist's Top of the List, 1994

17.5 Carter, Jimmy. **Talking Peace: A Vision for the Next Generation.** Dutton Children's Books, 1993. ISBN 0-525-44959-0.

Former president Jimmy Carter offers "A Vision for the Next Generation" that stresses "talking as well as acting peace." Carter provides historical background to many of today's widespread global conflicts. At the end of the book, he suggests how young people can make a difference—not only locally, but on a larger scale.

17.6 Cohen, Daniel. **Cults.** Milbrook Press, 1994. ISBN 1-56294-324-3.

Daniel Cohen takes readers inside various cults to see what really happens on a day-to-day basis. He provides dramatic description of the events surrounding the burning of the Branch Davidian compound in Waco, Texas, and the mass suicides in Jonestown, Guyana. The message is ultimately reassuring—none of the cults described is as widespread or as powerful as their leadership would like us to believe. Cohen reaffirms that as long as individuals refuse to surrender their critical judgment and can think for themselves, there is no danger of falling prey to a cult.

17.7 Fine, John Christopher. **Racket Squad.** Atheneum, 1993. ISBN 0-689-31569-4.

Did you know that organized crime allegedly controls the toxic waste business? Or that many designer products are illegal counterfeits? After years as a New York prosecutor investigating organized crime, John Christopher Fine writes about this world that thrives below the surface of the city. Reputed underworld crime figures like Joe Colombo and Anthony "Fat Tony" Salerno take on infamous lives in this account. Much of what the author describes is still happening today.

17.8 Gottfried, Ted. **Privacy: Individual Right v. Social Needs.** Millbrook Press, 1994. ISBN 1-56294-403-7.

Many people say that the media and modern technology invade almost every aspect of our private lives today. Consider the use of bugging devices, camcorders, mandated drug testing for employment, computer data banks, and even locker searches. Is privacy a *right* or a *privilege*? Under what circumstances should we surrender our privacy? Ted Gottfried discusses both sides of the problem of maintaining our personal lives in an ever more intrusive world.

17.9   Graff, Nancy Price. **Where the River Runs: A Portrait of a Refugee Family.** Photographs by Richard Howard. Little, Brown, 1993. ISBN 0-316-32287-3.

This account of a Cambodian refugee family in Cambridge, Massachusetts, opens on Thanksgiving Day with a reminder of the pilgrims who came to America to build a better life. Sohka Prek and her three sons are attempting to adjust to a modern American life and at the same time maintain a firm hold on their Cambodian heritage. Superb photographs and simple language give readers a close look at this family during a typical day of school and work, visiting their grandmother, shopping, and celebrating holidays. *Multicultural.*

17.10   Granfield, Linda. **Cowboy: An Album.** Illustrated by Seth. Ticknor and Fields, 1994. ISBN 0-395-68430-7.

Ever wonder how realistically cowboys are portrayed in song, prose, and film? *Cowboy: An Album* tells all: the dirt, customs, boredom, trappings, danger, uncertainty of employment, and certainty of early retirement. Photographs and archival illustrations bring to life cowboys of myth and media as well as those real mavericks from varying ethnic backgrounds. Some noteworthy cowboys and cowgirls are profiled. Included are lexicons and a list of suggested reading. Wild West enthusiasts will love this book.

17.11   Kerson, Adrian. **Terror in the Towers: Amazing Stories from the World Trade Center Disaster.** Random House, 1993. ISBN 0-679-85332-4.

The 1993 bombing of New York's World Trade Center shocked the nation. Here is an account of the event that reveals the mysterious duality of human nature: from an act of cowardly terrorism came so many gestures of valor. These are the stories of office workers baffled by a communication system failure, kindergarten students trapped in an elevator for hours, a disabled man carried down hundreds of stairs by co-workers, and rescuers who fight tirelessly to save thousands of lives.

17.12   Layden, Joe. **Domestic Violence.** Millbrook Press, 1994. ISBN 1-56294-554-8.

More American women die annually as a result of domestic violence than from disease or accidents. Almost 4 percent of American children are abused or neglected. Profiles of the typical abuser and victim emphasize that domestic abuse is not limited to specific social, economic, ethnic, or age groups but pervades American society. "Breaking Free," a concluding chapter in this book in the Headliners series, offers information about groups actively working to break the cycle of abusive domestic violence.

17.13   Meltzer, Milton. **Cheap Raw Material.** Viking, 1994. ISBN 0-670-83128-X.

Children have been "cheap raw material" from the days of the ancient Roman slave trade to today's fast-food industry. This book chronicles historical and present-day realities of child labor. Firsthand accounts from child workers are skillfully integrated with shocking statistics about the invisible underaged and underpaid workers in our world. Employment laws and regulations are presented, as well as a question-and-answer section designed to help the working teen.

17.14   Rappaport, Doreen. **The Alger Hiss Trial.** HarperCollins/Harper Trophy Books, 1993. ISBN 0-06-446115-7.

In this volume in the Be the Judge/Be the Jury series, the reader must decide whether alleged Communist spy Alger Hiss was a traitor to the U.S. government. Author Doreen Rappaport presents pertinent evidence from the 1948 trial records, commenting objectively on our legal system as she proceeds through defense and prosecution arguments. Here is a startling lesson in American history, where the reader must evaluate the case and decide the outcome.

17.15   Rappaport, Doreen. **Tinker vs. Des Moines: Student Rights on Trial.** HarperCollins/Harper Trophy Books, 1993. ISBN 0-06-446114-9.

To support a truce and to mourn the dead on both sides in the Vietnam War, some Iowa students wore black arm bands to school one day in 1965 and were suspended. Three of the students sued school officials in the case known as *Tinker vs. Des Moines.* This landmark case went all the way to the Supreme Court. Follow and evaluate the process of the trial in this book in the Be the Judge/Be the Jury series. Review the background, documents, newspaper headlines, and photographs; then, *you* decide: guilty or not guilty?

17.16   Sherrow, Victoria. **The U.S. Health Care Crisis: The Fight over Access, Quality, and Cost.** Millbrook Press, 1994. ISBN 1-56294-364-2.

With skyrocketing medical costs and more than 37 million people uninsured, the United States has begun to grapple with the problem of health care reform. Victoria Sherrow explains how our basic approach to medicine has led to conflicting solutions to this problem. She handles a controversial subject in a straightforward manner, giving particular attention to issues of access, quality, and cost. Most Americans agree that something must be done. Readers of this book will be ready to enter the debate.

17.17   Sutton, Roger. **Hearing Us Out: Voices from the Gay and Lesbian Community.** Photographs by Lisa Ebright. Little, Brown, 1994. ISBN 0-316-82326-0.

Growing up gay often means growing up confused and in search of information. It can also mean growing up isolated, sometimes desperate and even suicidal. In moving first-person accounts, the individuals interviewed for this book tell their stories. How do they deal with marriage, child adoption, the devastating reality of AIDS? These voices portray the gay and lesbian community as a proud and diverse group.

18 Sports

18.1 Brashler, William. **The Story of Negro League Baseball.** Ticknor and Fields, 1994. ISBN 0-395-69721-2.

They are dynamic baseball players, excellent hitters, extraordinary pitchers, with proven records of unbelievable talent. Anybody's dream team can be chosen from their ranks, but no major league baseball team in America will have them. Why? They are black men. Through firsthand accounts, Rashler re-creates a great but tragic era from 1887 until 1947 when blacks were excluded from major league baseball, forced to create their own teams and leagues in order to play a sport they loved. *Multicultural.*

18.2 Christopher, Matt. **Man Out at First.** Illustrated by Ellen Beier. Little, Brown, 1993. ISBN 0-316-14084-8.

Eight-year-old Turtleneck Jones enjoys playing baseball, especially since he is pretty good and gets to play first base. Unfortunately, Turtleneck is knocked unconscious when a ball thrown by Bus Mercer hits him in the chest. His friends tease him about fainting; Bus seems to be avoiding him; and his coach will not let him play. Turtleneck considers giving up baseball, but then he receives some sound advice from his visually impaired neighbor.

18.3 Christopher, Matt. **Pressure Play.** Illustrated by Karin Lidbecki. Little, Brown, 1993. ISBN 0-316-14098-8.

Travis Bonelli has two interests—playing baseball and editing horror movies onto videotape. When he moves to a new town, he becomes the shortstop on the baseball team and enters a contest for the best videotape of horror film clips. However, strange things begin to happen. He receives a series of anonymous telephone threats to improve his play—or else, and his videotapes disappear. Travis is under pressure to solve the mysteries and help his team win the playoff series.

18.4 Christopher, Matt. **Top Wing.** Illustrated by Marcy Ramsey. Little, Brown, 1994. ISBN 0-316-14099-6.

Team cohesion falls apart for the Anchors after Dana's father saves Benton from a disastrous house fire. Dana cannot understand why his old soccer buddy is ignoring him on the field and in school until he begins to unravel the mysteries of how the fire started and why Benton continues to suffer from smoke inhalation. Matt Christopher weaves together messages about friendship, sportsmanship, and the hazards of smoking.

18.5   Deuker, Carl. **Heart of a Champion.** Little, Brown, 1993. ISBN 0-316-18166-8.

Still hurting from the unexpected death of his father, Seth dives head-long into baseball and friendship with Jimmy. Committed to becoming the best baseball players possible, the two friends grow up developing their skills and dreams together. This once-in-a-lifetime friendship allows Seth to discover who he really is and Jimmy to choose who he wants to be as they experience the complexities and triumphs of winning and losing.

ALA Best Books for Young Adults, 1994
ALA Quick Picks for Young Adults, 1994

18.6   Dygard, Thomas J. **Game Plan.** Morrow Junior Books, 1993. ISBN 0-688-12007-5.

When the coach of Barton High's football team is injured in a car accident, the only person able to replace him for the final season game is Hubert "Beano" Hatton, student manager. Beano is great in calculus and English, but does he have the right stuff to coach the team's temperamental players and lead Barton High to victory? Beano soon discovers his own powers of intuition and common sense in this fast-paced sports novel.

18.7   Gutman, Dan. **World Series Classics.** Viking, 1994. ISBN 0-670-85286-4.

Baseball fans will enjoy this play-by-play commentary on the five most exciting World Series championship games from 1912 to 1991. In a detailed account of each game, Dan Gutman highlights individual players, newspaper reviews, photographs, anecdotes, statistics, and even the ball park weather to re-create the suspense of the actual game. The true baseball fan will love this trip through baseball history, enjoying photographs and box score charts as the games unfold.

18.8   Hughes, Dean, and Tom Hughes. **Baseball Tips.** Illustrated by Dennis Lyall. Random House, 1993. ISBN 0-679-83642-X.

What do baseball coaches everywhere stress most of the time? The *basics*. This indexed book covers such baseball basics as hitting, bunting, stealing, throwing, and fielding. Included are practice drills and a glossary of terms. Illustrations effectively support the text, including excellent line drawings of field positions. Coaches and managers alike would be delighted if all their players read this book.

18.9   Kramer, S. A. **Adventure in Alaska: An Amazing True Story of the World's Longest, Toughest Dog Sled Race.** Random House/Bullseye Books, 1993. ISBN 0-679-94511-3.

This book in the Read It to Believe It series is the fascinating, true account of Libby Riddles and her faithful dogsled team, the first woman to win the grueling 1,200-mile Iditarod Trail race from Anchorage to Nome, Alaska, in 1985. Riddles encountered freezing blizzards, moose attacks, runaway dogsleds, disorientation, and collisions with walls of ice and snow before she finally beat the odds and won the race. Her story is an inspiration to athletes, women, and animal lovers alike.

18.10   Lipsyte, Robert. **The Chief.** HarperCollins, 1993. ISBN 0-06-021064-8.

In this sequel to *The Brave,* Sonny Bear, a Moscondoga Indian, has what it takes to be the next heavyweight boxing champion. However, he must decide where his loyalties lie: the false lure of fame in Las Vegas and Hollywood; the people of his Moscondoga Nation as they battle over a gaming casino on their reservation; or his friendship with fledgling writer Martin Malcolm Witherspoon, the narrator of this brisk and riveting sports novel. Can Sonny Bear handle all this pressure and still emerge a winner? See also Ted Lewin's autobiography, *I Was a Teenage Professional Wrestler* (3.14), as a companion book. *Multicultural.*

18.11   Lynch, Chris. **Shadow Boxer.** HarperCollins, 1993. ISBN 0-06-023027-4.

George has been the man of the family since his father died of boxing-related injuries. While he has tried to teach his younger brother how to fight, he has been unable to teach Monty how *not* to be a fighter. In accepting this heavy parental responsibility, George discovers that he cannot protect his brother forever.

ALA Best Books for Young Adults, 1994

18.12   Neumann, Peter J. **Playing a Virginia Moon.** Houghton Mifflin, 1994. ISBN 0-395-66562-0.

Chet Tralek has run 1,000 miles this summer preparing for the cross-country season. Nothing has ever been as important to him as beating the school record. But the challenge is complicated by Maggie's flirting and Johnny Fiske's speed. How to use his anger? How to push the pace? Chet wonders if he will ever be successful at anything important in his life.

18.13   Savage, Deborah. **To Race a Dream.** Houghton Mifflin, 1994. ISBN 0-395-69252-0.

Fifteen-year-old Theodora Harris dreams of driving the powerful horses on a harness-racing farm near her home. She faces two obstacles: she is a girl, and the year is 1906; rough sports like horse racing are unthinkable for women in this era. Undaunted by these barriers, Theodora disguises herself as Theo and gains entry to the world of racing. Along the way she finds love as well as the courage to pursue her real dream.

18.14   Schleifer, Jay. **Firebird: Built with Excitement!** Crestwood House, 1993. ISBN 0-89686-702-1.

For years, Pontiac's motto has been "We Build Excitement!" Most fans who drive Firebirds believe the auto company has delivered on their slogan. What today's teens might not know is that the Firebird division used to be General Motors' dullest division. In this history of the Firebird, readers can see changes that have occurred in the styling and performance of this car over the past forty years. Learn, too, about plans for the next generation of Firebirds in this book in the Cool Classics series.

18.15   Schleifer, Jay. **Lamborghini: Italy's Raging Bull.** Crestwood House, 1993. ISBN 0-89686-698-X.

Ferruccio Lamborghini originally was a successful builder of tractors. He loved sports cars and bought an Italian model that had some problems; so Lamborghini decided he could build a better automobile. This book details the development of Bizzarini's magnificent V-12 engine and various Lamborghini models including the Miura, Countach, and a 200 m.p.h. road car, the Diablo. There is even a chapter on the "Rambo Lambo," a four-wheel-drive vehicle. If you like exotic sports cars, this volume in the Cool Classics series is the book for you.

18.16   Walker, Paul Robert. **The Sluggers Club: A Sports Mystery.** Harcourt Brace, 1993. ISBN 0-15-276163-2.

Some baseball equipment is suddenly missing. Twelve-year-old baseball enthusiast B. J. and two other Little Leaguers, Wash and Tony, decide to form the Sluggers Club to find out what is happening. The boys face scary and embarrassing situations as they pursue their list of suspects. The situation becomes more desperate when their team, the Halbertson's Flowers, goes into a batting slump just before the championship game.

18.17   Weaver, Will. **Striking Out.** HarperCollins, 1993. ISBN 0-06-023346-X.

As Billy Bagg knows well, life on a Minnesota dairy farm is full of hard work. But Billy is a natural athlete who can play baseball like a dream. As baseball becomes his dream, he faces increasing conflict with his father, who needs Billy's help on the farm, especially after the death of Billy's older brother. Baseball teaches Billy about tough choices and decisions that can change your life forever.

ALA Best Books for Young Adults, 1994

19 Supernatural

19.1 Bauer, Marion Dane. **A Taste of Smoke.** Houghton Mifflin/Clarion Books, 1993. ISBN 0-395-64341-4.

Caitlin has been waiting all year for her sister, Pam, to get home from college. They have planned for just the two of them to go camping for three days. But first Alex, a friend of Pam's from college, shows up and joins them, disturbing Caitlin's plans. Then Frank appears, a young boy strangely dressed and almost too eager to be Caitlin's friend. What does he want from her, and why can't anyone else see him? Or can they?

19.2 Bellairs, John. **The Drum, the Doll, and the Zombie.** Dial Books, 1994. ISBN 0-8037-1462-9.

Thirteen-year-old Johnny Dixon and his neighbor, Professor Childermass, have a party for an old friend, Dr. Coote, a professor of folklore. Everyone laughs when Dr. Coote begins to talk about his research on voodoo and zombies—until he shows them a mysterious drum that seems to have magical powers. From that moment, their lives are imperiled as they encounter Mama Sinestra and her evil powers. Will their spells overcome the black magic of the drum, the doll, and the zombie?

19.3 Carmody, Isobelle. **The Gathering.** Dial Books, 1994. ISBN 0-8037-1716-4.

Nathaniel is tired of changing schools and towns. Trying to adjust to losing a father is hard enough without moving around so much. Now he and his mother have moved to Cheshunt, supposedly a model community, but something is definitely wrong. The students and staff at Three North High are distant, secretive, and menacing; the school youth group, called the Gathering, is led by sinister Mr. Karle, the vice principal. Why would anyone build a school next to a slaughterhouse? Nathaniel joins a circle of teenagers determined to stand up to the forces of darkness that have overpowered the school and the community. Originally published in Australia.

19.4   Elfman, Eric. **The Very Scary Almanac.** Random House, 1993. ISBN 0-679-84401-5.

Have you ever wondered how to protect yourself from a vampire, whether witches really need broomsticks to fly, or what should be included in a ghost hunter's kit? If so, then this is the handbook for you. In this collection of scary facts, Eric Elfman discusses ghouls, curses, poltergeists, aliens, mysterious creatures, heinous humans, and a multitude of other frightening topics. Don't read this one before bedtime!

19.5   Gilden, Mel. **The Pumpkins of Time.** Harcourt Brace/Browndeer Press, 1994. ISBN 0-15-200889-6.

Since Uncle Hugo began his experiments with dandelions as a way to stop time, fourteen-year-old Myron's life has been marked by a series of explosions. Myron and his friend, Princess, see dandelion mush as a way of preserving Myron's antique comic book collection. However, when the menacing alien from outer space arrives, Myron and Princess find themselves "exploded" forward and backward in time, not knowing why.

19.6   Piazza, Linda. **Call of the Deep.** Avon Books, 1994. ISBN 0-380-77330-9.

The stretch of beach in front of the cabin is deserted, except for one figure who calls from the darkness: "Come. Take my hand. Come walk into the water with me." Delia is terrified, both by the deadly power of the raging surf and by the mysterious force that draws her into the arms of the dark-eyed stranger. Yet she is powerless to resist.

19.7   Rau, Margaret. **World's Scariest "True" Ghost Stories.** Sterling, 1994. ISBN 0-8069-0796-7.

These twenty-eight very short ghost stories will amaze and mystify you. Read, for example, about a strange dog that grows bigger at each sighting; about a long-dead Royal Air Force aviator who still flies his phantom biplane; or about a murderous "presence" that awaits its victims in an old gabled house. Collected from all parts of the world, these stories are guaranteed to make you shiver!

19.8   Reiss, Kathryn. **Dreadful Sorry.** Harcourt Brace Jovanovich, 1993. ISBN 0-15-224213-9.

"You're on drugs or else stark-raving loony!" That's what people think when Molly tries to explain her recurring nightmare of drowning, or the waking dreams where she slips into the life of a young woman who disappeared more than eighty years before. Molly cannot seem to shake the haunting melody that keeps running through her head, and the face she sees in the mirror is not always her own.

19.9   Reiss, Kathryn. **Pale Phoenix.** Harcourt Brace, 1994. ISBN 0-15-200030-5.

Miranda is puzzled by runaway orphan Abby Chandler, a sullen girl that Miranda's parents have taken in. Once, while Miranda follows her through the snow, Abby's tracks disappear abruptly. Who is this girl, with her collection of old photographs and sheet music, who can disappear into thin air? Where does she go and why? *Pale Phoenix* is the story of a young woman's secret and horrible link to the past.

19.10 Sinykin, Sheri Cooper. **Sirens.** Lothrop, Lee and Shepard, 1993. ISBN 0-688-12309-0.

Chantal's life is mysteriously changed when she accepts the statue of a sea queen from an old sculptor. Suddenly Chantal hears distant singing and ethereal music. Moreover, strange accidents begin to happen to the boys she knows. This novel draws on stories from Homer's *Odyssey* and the myth of the Lorelei, the nymph whose singing lured sailors to their deaths in ancient times. It weaves a mystery that Chantal must solve if she is to save her friends' lives, and possibly even her own.

19.11 Wyss, Thelma Hatch. **A Stranger Here.** HarperCollins, 1993. ISBN 0-06-021438-4.

For sixteen-year-old Jada Sinclair, taking care of a sick aunt in Idaho is not her idea of a fun summer vacation. However, as she begins to rummage around in the attic of her aunt's Victorian house, she encounters an antique dress, an old record player, and a ghost from World War II who died the day Jada was born. Jada befriends the ghost, and in the process, she makes new discoveries about friendship, about life's golden moments, and about her own spirit.

Appendix: Award-Winning Books

Among the many ways for finding good books to read are the following awards and recognitions. We have included major awards given to books for young readers from 1993 to 1995, as well as information about some other useful booklists.

Jane Addams Award

The Jane Addams Award, established in 1953, is given annually to the book for young people that most effectively promotes peace, social justice, world community, or equality of the sexes and of all races. It is given by the Women's International League for Peace and Freedom and the Jane Addams Peace Association.

1993 Temple, Frances. *Taste of Salt: A Story of Modern Haiti*. Orchard Books.

1994 Levine, Ellen. *Freedom's Children: Young Civil Rights Activists Tell Their Own Stories*. Avon Books.

1995 Freedman, Russell. *Kids at Work: Lewis Hine and the Crusade against Child Labor*. Clarion Books, 1994.

Booklist's Top of the List

The "Top of the List," initiated in 1991, represents the selections made by the staff of *Booklist* of the very best of their "Editor's Choice" annual lists. The complete "Editor's Choice" lists may be found in *Booklist* each January 15.

1993 **Youth Fiction**
Wolff, Virginia Euwer. *Make Lemonade*. Henry Holt.
Youth Nonfiction
Appelbaum, Diana. *Giants in the Land*. Illustrated by Michael McCurdy. Houghton Mifflin.
Youth Picture Book
Erlich, Amy. *Parents in the Pigpen, Pigs in the Tub*. Illustrated by Steven Kellogg. Dial.

1994 **Youth Fiction**
Temple, Frances. *The Ramsay Scallop*. Orchard Books/Richard Jackson.
Youth Nonfiction
Bachrach, Susan D. *Tell Them We Remember: The Story of the Holocaust*. Little, Brown.

Youth Picture Book
Guback, Georgie. *Luka's Quilt.* Greenwillow.

Boston Globe–Horn Book Award

Given annually since 1967 by the *Boston Globe* and *Horn Book Magazine,* these awards are conferred in three categories: outstanding fiction or poetry, outstanding nonfiction, and outstanding picture book.

1993   **Fiction Award**
Berry, James. *Ajeemah and His Son.* HarperCollins.
Fiction Honor Book
Lowry, Lois. *The Giver.* Houghton Mifflin.
Nonfiction Award
McKissack, Patricia, and Fredrick McKissack. *Sojourner Truth: Ain't I a Woman?* Scholastic.
Nonfiction Honor Book
Krull, Kathleen. *Lives of the Musicians: Good Times, Bad Times (And What the Neighbors Thought).* Harcourt Brace.
Picture Book Award
Alexander, Lloyd. *The Fortune-Tellers.* Illustrated by Trina Schart Hyman. Dutton Children's Books.
Picture Book Honor Books
McDermott, Gerald. *Raven: A Trickster Tale from the Pacific Northwest.* Illustrated by the author. Harcourt Brace.
Sis, Peter. *Komodo!* Greenwillow Books.

1994   **Fiction Award**
Williams, Vera B. *Scooter.* Illustrated by the author. Greenwillow Books.
Fiction Honor Books
Fine, Anne. *Flour Babies.* Little, Brown.
Fox, Paula. *Western Wind.* Orchard Books.
Nonfiction Award
Freedman, Russell. *Eleanor Roosevelt: A Life of Discovery.* Houghton Mifflin/ Clarion Books.
Nonfiction Honor Books
Marrin, Albert. *Unconditional Surrender: U. S. Grant and the Civil War.* Atheneum.
Levy, Constance. *A Tree Place, and Other Poems.* Illustrated by Robert Sabuda. Macmillan/Margaret K. McElderry Books.
Picture Book Award
Say, Allen. *Grandfather's Journey.* Illustrated by the author. Houghton Mifflin.
Picture Book Honor Books
Henkes, Kevin. *Owen.* Illustrated by the author. Greenwillow Books.
Sis, Peter. *A Small Tall Tale from the Far Far North.* Illustrated by the author. Alfred A. Knopf.

Andrew Carnegie Medal

This medal, first given in 1937 to commemorate the hundredth anniversary of the birth of Andrew Carnegie, is awarded annually by the British Library Association to an outstanding children's book written in English and first published in the United Kingdom.

1993 Fine, Anne. *Flour Babies*. Hamish Hamilton.
1994 Swindells, Robert. *Stone Cold*. Hamish Hamilton.

International Board on Books for Young People Honor List

Established in 1956, this list is published every two years to recognize books published in countries all over the world that represent the best in literature for young readers. Listed below is the most recent honoree from the United States.

1994 Paterson, Katherine. *Lyddie*. E. P. Dutton.

International Reading Association Children's Book Award

Given annually since 1975, this award honors the first or second book of an author, from any country, who shows unusual promise.

1993 Hesse, Karen. *Letters from Rifka*. Henry Holt.
1994 Toll, Nelly. *Behind the Secret Window: A Memoir of a Hidden Childhood during World War Two*. Dial Books.
1995 Krisher, Trudy. *Spite Fences*. Delacorte Press.
       Bowen, Gary. *Stranded at Plimouth Plantation*. HarperCollins.

Coretta Scott King Award

These awards and honor designations have been given annually since 1969 to African American authors and illustrators for books that are outstanding inspirational and educational contributions to literature for children and young people. They are given by the Social Responsibilities Round Table of the American Library Association.

1993 **Author Award**
       McKissack, Patricia C. *The Dark-Thirty: Southern Tales of the Supernatural*. Illustrated by Brian Pinkney. Alfred A. Knopf.
       Illustrator Award
       Anderson, David A./Sankofa, reteller. *The Origin of Life on Earth: An African Creation Myth*. Illustrated by Kathleen Atkins Wilson. Sight Productions.

1994 **Author Award**
       Johnson, Angela. *Toning the Sweep*. Orchard Books.
       Author Honor Books
       Thomas, Joyce Carol. *Brown Honey in Broomwheat Tea*. Illustrated by Floyd Cooper. HarperCollins.
       Myers, Walter Dean. *Malcolm X: By Any Means Necessary*. Scholastic.
       Illustrator Award
       Feelings, Tom. *Soul Looks Back in Wonder*. Illustrated by the author. Doubleday.
       Illustrator Honor Books
       Thomas, Joyce Carol. *Brown Honey in Broomwheat Tea*. Illustrated by Floyd Cooper. HarperCollins.

Mitchell, Margaree King. *Uncle Jed's Barbershop.* Illustrated by James Ransome. Simon and Schuster.

1995 **Author Award**

McKissack, Patricia C., and Fredrick L. McKissack. *Christmas in the Big House, Christmas in the Quarters.* Scholastic.

Author Honor Books

Woodson, Jacqueline. *I Hadn't Meant to Tell You This.* Delacorte Press.

McKissack, Patricia C., and Fredrick McKissack. *Black Diamond: The Story of the Negro Baseball League.* Scholastic.

Illustrator Award

Johnson, James Weldon. *The Creation.* Illustrated by James E. Ransome. Holiday House.

Illustrator Honor Books

Medearis, Angela Shelf. *The Singing Man.* Illustrated by Terea Shaffer. Holiday House.

Grimes, Nikki. *Meet Danitra Brown.* Illustrated by Floyd Cooper. Lothrop, Lee and Shepard Books.

NCTE Orbis Pictus Award for Outstanding Nonfiction for Children

This award commemorates the work of John Comenius, *Orbis Pictus: The World in Pictures,* published in 1657 and historically considered to be the first book actually planned for young readers. The selection committee chooses one outstanding nonfiction book each year on the basis of accuracy, organization, design, writing style, and usefulness for classroom teaching.

1993 **Award**

Stanley, Jerry. *Children of the Dust Bowl: The True Story of the School at Weedpatch Camp.* Crown.

Honor Books

Cummings, Pat, ed. *Talking with Artists.* Macmillan/Bradbury Press.

Cone, Molly. *Come Back, Salmon: How a Group of Dedicated Kids Adopted Pigeon Creek and Brought It Back to Life.* Sierra Club Books.

1994 **Award**

Murphy, Jim. *Across America on an Emigrant Train.* Houghton Mifflin/Clarion Books.

Honor Books

Brandenburg, Jim. *To the Top of the World: Adventures with Arctic Wolves.* Walker.

Brooks, Bruce. *Making Sense: Animal Perception and Communication.* Farrar, Straus and Giroux.

1995 **Award**

Swanson, Diane. *Safari beneath the Sea: The Wonder World of the North Pacific Coast.* Sierra Club Books.

Honor Books

Dewey, Jennifer Owings. *Wildlife Rescue: The Work of Dr. Kathleen Ramsay.* Boyds Mills Press.

Freedman, Russell. *Kids at Work: Lewis Hine and the Crusade against Child Labor.* Houghton Mifflin/Clarion Books.

McKissack, Patricia C., and Fredrick L. McKissack. *Christmas in the Big House, Christmas in the Quarters.* Scholastic.

NCTE Award for Excellence in Poetry for Children

Established in 1977, this award is presented every three years to a living American poet for an aggregate body of work for children ages three to thirteen.

1994 Barbara Esbensen. Major works: *Cold Stars and Fireflies: Poems for the Four Seasons* (1984, HarperCollins); *Words with Wrinkled Knees* (1987, HarperCollins); and *Who Shrank My Grandmother's House? Poems of Discovery* (1992, HarperCollins).

John Newbery Medal

The Newbery Medal and honor book designations have been given annually since 1922 to the most distinguished contributions to literature for young readers published in the United States during the preceding year. The authors must be citizens or residents of the United States. The award is given by the Association for Library Service to Children of the American Library Association.

1993 **Medal**
      Rylant, Cynthia. *Missing May.* Orchard Books.
      Honor Books
      Brooks, Bruce. *What Hearts.* HarperCollins.
      McKissack, Patricia C. *The Dark-Thirty: Southern Tales of the Supernatural.* Illustrated by Brian Pinkney. Alfred A. Knopf.
      Myers, Walter Dean. *Somewhere in the Darkness.* Scholastic.

1994 **Medal**
      Lowry, Lois. *The Giver.* Houghton Mifflin.
      Honor Books
      Conly, Jane Leslie. *Crazy Lady!* HarperCollins.
      Freedman, Russell. *Eleanor Roosevelt: A Life of Discovery.* Houghton Mifflin/Clarion Books.
      Yep, Laurence. *Dragon's Gate.* HarperCollins.

1995 **Medal**
      Creech, Sharon. *Walk Two Moons.* HarperCollins.
      Honor Books
      Cushman, Karen. *Catherine, Called Birdy.* Houghton Mifflin/Clarion Books.
      Farmer, Nancy. *The Ear, the Eye and the Arm.* Orchard Books.

Edgar Allan Poe/Mystery Writers of America Award for Juvenile Mystery

The Mystery Writers of America have given awards for the best juvenile and best young adult mysteries every year since 1961. Each winner receives an

"Edgar," a ceramic bust of Edgar Allan Poe, who was one of the originators of the mystery story.

1993 **Best Juvenile Novel**
Bunting, Eve. *Coffin on a Case.* HarperCollins Children's Books.
Best Young Adult Novel
Reaver, Chap. *A Little Bit Dead.* Delacorte.

1994 **Best Juvenile Novel**
Wallace, Barbara Brooks. *The Twin in the Tavern.* Atheneum.
Best Young Adult Novel
Nixon, Joan Lowery. *The Name of the Game Was Murder.* Delacorte.

1995 **Best Juvenile Novel**
Roberts, Willo Davis. *The Absolutely True Story . . . How I Visited Yellowstone Park with the Terrible Rubes.* Atheneum.
Best Young Adult Novel
Springer, Nancy. *Toughing It.* Harcourt Brace.

Booklists

In addition to recognition awarded to a handful of selected titles, several organizations issue annual lists of recommended books. While such lists are too lengthy to include in this volume, we include descriptions of the booklists that would be of interest to readers of *High Interest—Easy Reading* and indicate how to obtain these booklists.

American Library Association/Notable Children's Book Committee

The Notable Children's Book Committee of the Association for Library Service to Children, a division of the American Library Association, selects notable books each year on the basis of literary quality, originality of text and illustrations, design, format, subject matter of interest and value to children, and likelihood of acceptance by children. The complete list of Notable Books for Children appears yearly in the March 15 issue of *Booklist,* a journal published by the American Library Association.

American Library Association/Young Adult Library Services Association

The Young Adult Library Services Association of the American Library Association each year puts out a list of books with high appeal to young adult readers who, for whatever reason, do not like to read. The complete list of Quick Picks for Young Adults is published each year in the April 1 issue of *Booklist.* The association also puts out its list of Best Books for Young Adults every year, containing the fiction and nonfiction titles that show both high literary quality and popular appeal to young adult readers. The complete list of Best Books for Young Adults can also be found each year in the April 1 issue of *Booklist.* Both lists can be ordered directly from the ALA. Please indicate which list you want and send a self-addressed stamped business-size envelope for each list to YALSA, 50 E. Huron Street, Chicago, IL 60611.

International Reading Association

The International Reading Association each year asks children, young adults, and teachers to vote on a list of books recommended by recognized sources such as *Booklist, Horn Book*, and *Journal of Reading*. The top vote-getters in each group are listed in IRA journals each year and may also be obtained from the IRA directly. The complete list of Children's Choices appears yearly in the November issue of *The Reading Teacher,* the Young Adults' Choices appear in the November issue of *Journal of Reading,* and the Teachers' Choices appear in the November issue of *The Reading Teacher.* Single copies of any of the lists may be obtained for a charge of $1.00 from The International Reading Association, Order Department, 800 Barksdale Road, P.O. Box 8139, Newark, DE 19714-8139.

Notable Children's Trade Books in the Field of Social Studies

A Book Review Committee appointed by the National Council for the Social Studies, in cooperation with the Children's Book Council, selects books published in the United States each year that (1) are written primarily for students in grades K–8, (2) emphasize human relations, (3) represent a diversity of groups and are senstitive to a broad range of cultural experiences, (4) present an original theme or a fresh slant on a traditional topic, (5) are easily readable and of high literary quality, and (6) have a pleasing format and, when appropriate, illustrations that enrich the text. The complete list of these notable books appears yearly in the April/May issue of *Social Education,* the journal of the National Council for the Social Studies. Single copies may be obtained at no charge by sending a stamped (3 oz.), self-addressed 6" x 9" envelope to the Children's Book Council, 568 Broadway, Suite 404, New York, NY 10012. (In 1994, the date on the list was changed to coincide with the current calendar year. Prior to 1994, the date on the list was for the previous calendar year, the year in which the books were published. Thus, while there is no list labeled Notable 1993 Children's Trade Books in the Field of Social Studies, there has been no interruption in the listing. The 1993 books appear on the 1994 list.)

Outstanding Science Trade Books for Children

Each year a book review panel appointed by the National Science Teachers Association and assembled in cooperation with the Children's Book Council selects a list of outstanding books for young readers that present substantial science content in a clear, accurate, and up-to-date way. Each book is also evaluated on its freedom from gender, ethnic, and socioeconomic bias, and on the quality of its presentation of material. The complete list of outstanding science books is published each spring in the March issue of *Science and Children.*

Reprints of the list can be ordered from the Children's Book Council, Attn: Outstanding Science Trade Books for Children, 568 Broadway, Suite 404, New York, NY 10012. Enclose a self-addressed 6" x 9" envelope with 78¢ postage and $2.00 cash or check for one copy; bulk copies may be ordered at 90¢ each for 2–19 copies or 75¢ each for 20 or more copies.

School Library Journal's Best Books

The Book Review Editors of *School Library Journal* annually choose the best among the thousands of new books for younger readers submitted to the journal for review during the preceding year. Books are selected on the basis of strong story line, clear presentation, high-quality illustration, and probable appeal to young readers. The complete list is published each year in the December issue of the journal.

Lists and descriptions of other awards, prizes, and lists can be found at the front of recent editions of *Children's Books in Print,* an annual publication of R. R. Bowker.

Directory of Publishers

Atheneum. Division of Macmillan, 866 Third Avenue, New York, NY 10022. Orders to: 100 Front Street, Box 500, Riverside, NJ 08075. 800-257-5755.

Avon Books. 1350 Avenue of the Americas, 2nd Floor, New York, NY 10019. Orders to: P.O. Box 767, Dresden, TN 38225. 800-223-0690.

Avon/Flare Books. See Avon Books.

Berkley Publishing Group. 200 Madison Avenue, New York, NY 10016. Distributed by Warner Publishing Services, 810 Seventh Avenue, New York, NY 10019. Orders to: P.O. Box 506, East Rutherford, NJ 07073. 800-223-0510.

Berkley/Jove Books. See Berkley Publishing Group.

Berkley/Perigee Books. See Berkley Publishing Group.

Berkley/Splash Books. See Berkley Publishing Group.

Children's Press. Division of Grolier, 5440 N. Cumberland Avenue, Chicago, IL 60656. 800-621-1115.

Crabtree. 350 Fifth Avenue, Suite 3308, New York, NY 10018. 800-387-7650.

Crestwood House. Division of Macmillan, 866 Third Avenue, New York, NY 10022. Orders to: 100 Front Street, Box 500, Riverside, NJ 08075. 800-257-5755.

Dial Books. Division of E. P. Dutton, 2 Park Avenue, New York, NY 10016. Orders to: Penguin USA, P.O. Box 120, Bergenfield, NJ 07621. 800-387-0600.

E. P. Dutton. Division of Penguin USA, 375 Hudson Street, New York, NY 10014. Orders to: P.O. Box 120, Bergenfield, NJ 07621-0120. 800-526-0275.

Dutton's Children's Books. See E. P. Dutton.

Dutton/Cobblehill Books. See E. P. Dutton.

Dutton/Lodestar Books. See E. P. Dutton.

Eakin Press. P.O. Drawer 90159, Austin, TX 78709-0159. 512-288-1771.

William B. Eerdmans. 255 Jefferson Avenue, SE, Grand Rapids, MI 49503. 800-253-7521.

Enslow. Bloy Street and Ramsey Avenue, Box 777, Hillside, NJ 07205. 800-398-2504.

Greenwillow Books. Division of William Morrow, 105 Madison Avenue, New York, NY 10016. Orders to: 39 Plymouth Street, P.O. Box 1219, Fairfield, NJ 07007. 800-843-9389.

Harcourt Brace. (Formerly Harcourt Brace Jovanovich.) 1250 Sixth Avenue, San Diego, CA 92101. Orders to: 6277 Sea Harbor Drive, Orlando, FL 32887. 800-346-8648.

Harcourt Brace/Browndeer Press. See Harcourt Brace.

Harcourt Brace/Gulliver Books. See Harcourt Brace.

Harcourt Brace/Gulliver Green Books. See Harcourt Brace.

Harcourt Brace/Harvest Books. See Harcourt Brace.

Harcourt Brace/Jane Yolen Books. See Harcourt Brace.

HarperCollins. 10 East 53rd Street, New York, NY 10022-5299. Orders to: 1000 Keystone Industrial Park, Scranton, PA 18512-4621. 800-242-7737.

HarperCollins Children's Books. See HarperCollins.

HarperCollins/Laura Geringer Books. See HarperCollins.

HarperCollins/Harper Trophy Books. See HarperCollins.

HarperCollins/Charlotte Zolotow Books. See HarperCollins.

Holiday House. 425 Madison Avenue, New York, NY 10017. 212-688-0085.

Houghton Mifflin. 1 Beacon Street, Boston, MA 02108. Orders to: Wayside Road, Burlington, MA 01803. 800-225-3362.

Houghton Mifflin/Clarion Books. See Houghton Mifflin.

Hyperion Books for Children. Imprint of Walt Disney Publishing Group, 114 Fifth Avenue, New York, NY 10011. Distributed by Little, Brown. Orders to: 200 West Street, Waltham, MA 02254. 800-343-9204.

Alfred A. Knopf. Subsidiary of Random House, 201 East 50th Street, New York, NY 10022. Orders to: 400 Hahn Road, Westminster, MD 21157. 800-733-3000.

Alfred A. Knopf/Borzoi Books. See Alfred A. Knopf.

Alfred A. Knopf/Dorling Kindersley. See Alfred A. Knopf.

Little, Brown. Division of Time Warner, 34 Beacon Street, Boston, MA 02108. Orders to: 200 West Street, Waltham, MA 02254. 800-343-9204.

Little, Brown/Arcade Books. See Little, Brown.

Little, Brown/Joy Street Books. See Little, Brown.

Lothrop, Lee and Shepard Books. Division of William Morrow, 105 Madison Avenue, New York, NY 10016. Orders to: 39 Plymouth Street, P.O. Box 1219, Fairfield, NJ 07007. 800-237-0657.

Macmillan. 866 Third Avenue, New York, NY 10022. Orders to: 100 Front Street, Box 500, Riverside, NJ 08075. 800-257-5755.

Millbrook Press. 2 Old New Milford Road, Brookfield, CT 06804. 203-740-2220.

William Morrow. 105 Madison Avenue, New York, NY 10016. Orders to: Wilmor Warehouse, P.O. Box 1219, 39 Plymouth Street, Fairfield, NJ 07007. 800-843-9389.

William Morrow/Beech Tree Books. See William Morrow.

William Morrow/Tambourine Books. See William Morrow.

Morrow Junior Books. See William Morrow.

North-South Books. 1133 Broadway, Suite 1016, New York, NY 10010. Orders to: Picture Book Studio, 10 Central Street, Saxonville, MA 01701. 800-462-1252.

Orchard Books. Division of Franklin Watts, 95 Madison Avenue, 11th Floor, New York, NY 10016. 800-672-6672.

Oxford University Press. 200 Madison Avenue, New York, NY 10016. Orders to: 2001 Evans Road, Cary, NC 27513. 800-451-7556.

Random House. 210 East 50th Street, 31st Floor, New York, NY 10022. Orders to: 400 Hahn Road, Westminster, MD 21157. 800-733-3000.

Random House/Bullseye Books. See Random House.

Random House/Bullseye Chillers. See Random House.

Scholastic. 730 Broadway, New York, NY 10003. Orders to: P.O. Box 120, Bergenfield, NJ 07621. 800-325-6149.

Charles Scribner's Sons. Division of Macmillan, 866 Third Avenue, New York, NY 10022. Orders to: 100 Front Street, Box 500, Riverside, NJ 08075. 800-257-5755.

Sierra Club Books. 730 Polk Street, San Francisco, CA 94109. Distributed by Random House. Orders to: 400 Hahn Road, Westminster, MD 21157. 800-733-3000.

Sierra Club Books for Children. See Sierra Club Books.

Sterling Publishing. 387 Park Avenue South, New York, NY 10016-8810. 800-367-9692.

Gareth Stevens. River Center Building, 1555 N. River Center Drive, Suite 201, Milwaukee, WI 53212. 800-341-3569.

Ticknor and Fields. Affiliate of Houghton Mifflin, 215 Park Avenue South, New York, NY 10003. Orders to: Wayside Road, Burlington, MA 01803. 800-225-3362.

Troll Associates. Subsidiary of Educational Reading Services, 100 Corporate Drive, Mahwah, NJ 07430. 800-526-5289.

Troll Associates/Bridgewater Books. See Troll Associates.

Viking. Division of Penguin USA, 375 Hudson Street, New York, NY 10014. Orders to: P.O. Box 120, Bergenfield, NJ 07621-0120. 800-526-0275.

Walker and Company. 720 Fifth Avenue, New York, NY 10019. 800-289-2553.

Franklin Watts. Subsidiary of Grolier, 387 Park Avenue South, New York, NY 10016. Orders to: 5450 N. Cumberland Avenue, Chicago, IL 60657. 800-672-6672.

Franklin Watts/New England Aquarium. See Franklin Watts.

Franklin Watts/Cincinnati Zoo Books. See Franklin Watts.

Franklin Watts/First Books. See Franklin Watts.

Author Index

Subject Index

Title Index

Editor

Patricia Phelan is currently adjunct professor of English at Miramar Community College and supervises student teachers for the University of San Diego. She is a past chair of the Classroom Practices Committee and has served on the Secondary Section Steering Committee of NCTE. A fellow in the San Diego Area Writing Project, the California Literature Project, and the Humanities Institute, she has degrees in political science/English and education, with a specialization in reading. She has written curriculum for her school district, published in *English Journal* and NCTE affiliate journals, and completed twenty-eight years of secondary English teaching.

New from NCTE

YOUR READING
An Annotated Booklist for Middle School and Junior High
1995–96 Edition

Barbara G. Samuels and
G. Kylene Beers, editors
With a foreword by Joan Lowery Nixon

Whether your students want to read spine-tingling horror stories or speculations about future life in far-away galaxies, they are sure to find something to engage them in the latest edition of *Your Reading*. Covering young adult literature published in 1993 and 1994, the book contains over 1,200 annotations on topics from volcanos to oceans, compulsive gambling to anorexia, the joy of first love to the pain of breaking up and moving on. There's truly something for every interest. Since half of the annotations in *Your Reading* are on nonfiction subjects from fields like history, the natural and physical sciences, and current events, the book can be an important research tool for students working on school projects. A special feature of this edition is a list of 100 notable young adult books published during the 25 years prior to this edition of *Your Reading*, selected for their appeal to students in middle school and junior high. Author, title, and subject indexes and an appendix of award-winning books will help students locate books of interest; the detailed bibliographic information included with each entry and a directory of publishers' addresses and phone numbers will help them to track those books down. 381 pp. 1995. Grades 6–9. ISBN 0-8141-5943-5.
No. 59435-4024
$21.95 ($15.95 NCTE member price)

BOOKS FOR YOU
An Annotated Booklist for Senior High Students
1995 Edition

Leila Christenbury, editor
With a foreword by Jerry Spinelli

Whether your students are interested in space exploration or civil rights, love stories or mysteries, they are sure to find something in the 1995 edition of *Books for You* that will appeal to them. With over 1,000 titles included, there's something for every reader—and plenty for high school teachers and librarians to select from. The twenty-one reviewers—a diverse group of public and private school teachers, administrators, and librarians—selected these titles from some 5,000 received during the creation of *Books for You*. The books are grouped by subject into thirty-five thematic chapters, including "Adventure and Survival," "Dating and Sexual Awareness," "The Holocaust," and "Self-Help: Your Health and Your Body." More than 150 titles with a multicultural focus—each of which also appears in one of the topical chapters—are highlighted in an additional chapter called "Multicultural Themes." Every booklist entry includes full bibliographic information, a concise summary of the book's contents, and a notation about any awards the book has won. Author, title, and subject indexes will help readers locate a favorite author or find more books on a particular topic. An appendix that lists winners of major book awards and a directory of publishers are also included. 432 pp. 1995. Grades 9–12. ISBN 0-8141-0367-7.
No. 03677-4024
$21.95 ($15.95 NCTE member price)

National Council of Teachers of English
1111 W. Kenyon Road, Urbana, Illinois 61801-1096